The Complete UNOFFICIALL Guide to The Sopranos Seasons 5 and 6

By: Kristina Benson

The Complete Unofficial Guide to the Sopranos: Seasons 5 and 6

ISBN: 978-1-60332-047-4

Edited By: Brooke Winger

Copyright© 2008 Equity Press. No part of this publication may be reproduced, stored in a retrieval system, or transmitted in any form or by any means (electronic, mechanical, photocopying, recording or otherwise) without either the prior written permission of the publisher or a license permitting restricted copying in the United States or abroad.

The scanning, uploading and distribution of this book via the internet or via any other means without the permission of the publisher is illegal and punishable by law. Please purchase only authorized electronic editions, and do not participate in or encourage piracy of copyrighted materials.

Equity Press is not affiliated with HBO, Home Box Office, HBO subsidiaries, A&E, its creator David Chase, any HBO writers or directors.

Trademarks: All trademarks are the property of their respective owners. Equity Press is not associated with any product or vender mentioned in this book.

Printed in the United States of America

Table of Contents

Season 5 9

"Two Tonys" 11
Guest Starring 11
Synopsis 11
First Appearances 14
Hits 14
Trivia 14

"Rat Pack" 17
Guest Starring 17
Synopsis 18
First Appearances 19
Hits 19
Trivia 20

"Where's Johnny" 21
Guest Starring 21
Synopsis 22
Trivia 25

"All Happy Families" 27
Guest Starring 27
Synopsis 27
Hits 30
Trivia 30

"Irregular Around the Margins" 33
Guest Starring 33
Synopsis 34
First Appearances 36

"Sentimental Education" 37
   Guest Starring 37
   Synopsis.. 38

"In Camelot" 41
   Guest Starring 41
   Synopsis.. 42
   First Appearances 43
   Hits 43
   Trivia 44

"Marco Polo" 45
   Guest Starring 45
   Synopsis.. 45
   Hits 47
   Trivia 47

"Unidentified Black Males" 49
   Guest Starring 49
   Synopsis.. 50
   Trivia 51

"Cold Cuts" 53
   Guest Starring 53
   Synopsis.. 53
   First Apearances 55
   Trivia 55

"The Test Dream" 58
   Guest Starring 58
   Synopsis.. 59
   Hits 60
   Trivia 60

"Long Term Parking" 63
   Guest Starring 63
   Synopsis 64
   Hits 66
   Trivia 66

"All Due Respect" 67
   Guest Starring 67
   Synopsis 68
   Hits 70
   Trivia 70

Season 6 71

"Members Only" 73
   Guest Starring 73
   Synopsis 74
   First Appearances 75
   Hits 76
   Trivia 76

"Join the Club" 79
   Guest Starring 79
   Synopsis 79
   Trivia 82

"Mayham" 85
   Guest Starring 85
   Synopsis 86
   Hits 88
   Trivia 88

"The Fleshy Part of the Thigh" 91
    Guest Starring 91
    Synopsis... 91
    Hits 93
    Trivia 94

"Mr. And Mrs. John Sacrimoni Request"............... 95
    Guest starring.. 95
    Synopsis... 95
    Trivia 98

"Live Free or Die".. 99
    Guest Starring 99
    Synopsis... 99
    Trivia 102

"Luxury Lounge"... 105
    Guest Starring 105
    Synopsis... 106
    Hits 108

"Johnny Cakes" 109
    Guest Starring 109
    Synopsis... 109
    Trivia 111

"The Ride" 113
    Guest Starring 113
    Synopsis... 114
    Trivia 116

"Moe and Joe" 117
    Guest Starring 117
    Synopsis 118
    Hits 121
    Trivia 121

"Kaisha" 123
    Guest Starring 123
    Synopsis 124
    Trivia 130

INDEX 131

Season 5

"Two Tonys"

"Two Tonys" is the 53rd episode of the HBO original series, The Sopranos. It was the first episode for the show's fifth season. The episode was written by David Chase and Terence Winter and was directed by Tim Van Patten. It originally aired on Sunday March 7, 2004.

Guest Starring

- Robert Loggia as Michele "Feech" La Manna
- Frank Vincent as Phil Leotardo
- Joseph R. Gannascoli as Vito Spatafore
- Tony Lip as Carmine Lupertazzi
- Ray Abruzzo as Little Carmine
- Robert Funaro as Eugene Pontecorvo
- Arthur Nascarella as Carlo Gervasi
- George Loros as Raymond Curto
- Max Casella as Benny Fazio
- Carl Capotorto as Little Paulie Germani

Synopsis

Two years have passed since Tony and Carmela have separated, and Tony has moved into Livia's home. As the family is about to start dinner at Janice and Bobby's home—who are now married—the release of many mob associates that were convicted during the 1980s is covered on the news. The parolees include:

- Michele "Feech" La Manna, a respected and feared capo of the now dissolved La Manna crew.
- Tony Blundetto, Tony's cousin, who was an associate in the Soprano crew.
- Angelo Garepe, Carmine's former consigliere.
- Phil Leotardo, a captain in the New York family.

Tony is very happy about his cousin's release and is planning an over-the-top party when he gets home.

The following evening, while AJ is in the backyard, he discovers a large American Black Bear and calls for his mother for help. Carmela manages to drive the bear away and calls the police. The next day, the bear comes back and leaves shortly after. Tony then goes over to his former residence in order to express his concern for the welfare of Carmela and AJ. Carmela then tells Tony that he buys AJ too many gifts since he feels guilty about the separation. Tony then sends Benny Fazio and Little Paulie Germani to guard the backyard in case the bear comes back.

Meanwhile, Christopher and Paulie have a fight when Christopher recounts the "Pine Barrens" story in front of the capos, framing Paulie as the cause of the debacle. Paulie calls Christopher "Tony's little favorite" which offends Chris and they almost come to blows. Later, at comare night, Christopher forces Paulie to pay for dinner. At Satriale's the following morning, Paulie demands that Christopher return the money or begin to pay points, later, when in Atlantic City, telling everyone to choose whatever they want in order to inflate the bill for

Christopher. Paulie also sends over a very expensive bottle of wine to a table of unattractive women. The bill comes to $1184 and is given to Christopher, who leaves the waiter a $16.00 tip. Paulie and Christopher continue to bicker in the parking lot, until the waiter comes out to call them "fucking assholes", and Christopher throws a brick at him, hard, which hits him. The waiter then begins to convulse on the ground until Paulie shoots him. Paulie grabs the money as they both leave; the next day, Paulie and Christopher decide to bury the hatchet and make amends.

While Tony has lunch with Johnny Sack, Carmine and newly released Angelo Garepe, Carmine has a stroke and is taken to St. Vincent's Hospital. Little Carmine hears the news and books a flight on the next plane out of Miami. At the hospital, Johnny reminds Tony that he still has not forgotten about their sabotaged previous arrangement last year, which could have averted the current situation.

After watching The Prince of Tides, Tony begins thinking of Dr. Melfi and wishes to reconnect with her. When he calls her to set up a date, she tells him that she cannot date him to their previous clinical relationship. Tony then makes an appointment and confesses his love to her, but is again rebuffed. Tony makes a third attempt by giving her cruise tickets but when she tells him she does not like his values, he calls her a "fucking cunt". Tony then returns to the Soprano residence where he relieves Benny for the night and waits for the bear to come back.

First Appearances

- Feech La Manna: former capo of the now defunct La Manna crew who was incarcerated during the 1980s.
- Angelo Garepe: former Lupertazzi family consigliere.
- Phil Leotardo: (image only) former capo of Lupertazzi family.

Hits

- Raoul: An Atlantic City waiter who complained to Paulie and Christopher about a poor tip.

Trivia

- Tony attempts to demonstrate to Melfi that there are two Tony Sopranos, one of whom she has never seen before because their relationship was merely clinical.

- This could also be a reference to Tony and his cousin Tony Blundetto, who is released in this episode (though does not appear until the following episode)

- This episode is the first season opener where Tony is not featured picking up the newspaper from the driveway. Instead, Meadow runs the newspaper over with her car.

- Steve Buscemi (Tony Blundetto) is now billed in the opening credits. Jamie-Lynn Sigler is billed as "Jamie-Lynn DiScala" during this season.

"Rat Pack"

"Rat Pack" is the 54th episode of the HBO original series, The Sopranos. It was the 2nd episode for the show's fifth season. The episode was written by Matthew Weiner and was directed by Alan Taylor. It originally aired on March 14, 2004.

Guest Starring

- Robert Desiderio as Jack Massarone
- David Copeland as Joey Cogo
- Frank Vincent as Phil Leotardo
- Robert Loggia as Feech La Manna
- Rae Allen as Aunt Quintina Blundetto
- Vinny Vella as Jimmy Petrille
- Ray Aburzzo as Little Carmine
- Tony Lip as Carmine Lupertazzi
- Joe Santos as Angelo Garepe
- George Loros as Raymond Curto
- Frank Pellegrino as Bureau Chief Frank Cubitoso
- Matt Servitto as Agent Harris
- Frank Pando as Agent Grasso
- Lola Glaudini as Agent Deborah Ciccerone-Waldrup
- Karen Young as Agent Sanseverino
- Patti D'Arbanville as Lorraine Calluzzo
- Vanessa Ferlito as Tina Francesco

Synopsis

Tony gets together with contractor Jack Massarone at a small diner to discuss their business. Massarone presents him with a painting of Frank Sinatra, Dean Martin and Sammy Davis, Jr. and tries to get Tony to spill some of the beans about his connections of government officials. Tony avoids direct questioning even though he has no idea that Massarone is wearing a microphone in his hat, having flipped and joined Adriana and Raymond Curto as FBI cooperators. The latter two meet with agents, Adriana complaining about having to snitch on people and Raymond correcting inaudible snippets from a meeting he recorded.

At Tony Soprano's cousin's welcome home party, Tony tells the group how important his cousin was in his life growing up and explains how the family called him Tony-Uncle-Johnny and called his cousin Tony-Uncle-Al, a way of distinguishing the two boys by their fathers. Tony-Uncle-Al, aka Tony Blundetto, is not as keen on getting back in the business as his cousin would like him to be. Blundetto informs Tony that he was able to get an Associate's Degree in prison and is on his way to becoming a massage therapist. He wants to try have as normal a life as possible, and gets a job delivering linens.

Word comes from New York that Carmine Lupertazzi has passed way due to his stroke. During the funeral services, conflict arises between Little Carmine and Johnny Sack over rosary beads placed in his coffin. Little Carmine asserts that Ginny Sack placed Opus Dei beads in the coffin without asking him first, and also announces that he didn't mean the kind words he once said to Johnny.

Meanwhile, Adriana discovers an upside to being a government informant. When Tina Francesco, her purported best friend, flirts with Christopher one time too many, she tells Agent Sanseverino that Tina is an embezzler. Shortly thereafter, Tony finds out about Massarone's cooperation with the FBI and Massarone is found in the trunk of his car, a bullet hole in his head and a golf club cover in his mouth. On the Pulaski Skyway, Tony tosses the painting Massarone gave him out his car window.

First Appearances

- Tony Blundetto: Tony's cousin who was sent to jail in 1986 for hijacking a truck.
- Phil Leotardo: a capo in the Lupertazzi family.
- Lorraine Calluzzo: loan shark in the Lupertazzi family.

Hits

- Joseph "Joey" Cogo: killed prior in a payment dispute and deceased photos confirmed by Adriana.
- Carmine Lupertazzi: died of stroke
- Jack Massarone: Killed for being an FBI informant.

Trivia

- Jack Massarone gives Tony a painting of The Rat Pack.

- *Tina Francesco is the same Tina that was with Mustang Sally in the Season 3 episode "Another Toothpick".

"Where's Johnny"

"Where's Johnny?" is the 55th episode of the HBO original series, The Sopranos. It was the 3rd episode for the show's fifth season. The episode was written by Michael Caleo and was directed by John Patterson. It originally aired on March 21, 2004.

Guest Starring

- Frank Vincent as Phil Leotardo
- Robert Loggia as Feech La Manna
- Michael Cavalieri as E. Gary La Manna
- Anthony Desio as Jimmy La Manna
- Frances Ensemplare as Nucci Gualtieri
- Tony Lip as Carmine Lupertazzi
- Joe Santos as Angelo Garepe
- Karen Young as Agent Sanseverino
- Richard Portnow as Harold Melvoin
- Patti D'Arbanville as Lorraine Calluzzo
- Danielle Di Vecchio as Barbara Soprano Giglione
- Ed Vassalo as Tom Giglione

Synopsis

In New York, Phil Leotardo and Joe Peeps pay a visit to loan shark Lorraine Calluzzo and her boyfriend Jason in order to warn them that they will be "kicking up" directly to Johnny now. Lorraine says no, reminding them that she has always been faithful in giving her collections to Little Carmine in Miami. Phil Leotardo ties Lorraine up and fires a gun through a phone book that is held to her chest. The bullet only penetrates through to the middle of the phone book's "R" section. Phil then cautions her that "Next time, there'll be no next time!"

Lorraine and Jason then meets with Angelo Garepe, Tony and Junior at Harold Melvoin's office to discuss the New York issue. Lorraine tells Tony that she is frightened and that Johnny asked her to pay collections to him, Tony tries to resolve matters by recommending New York form an oligarchy of bosses: Johnny, Carmine and Angelo. Angelo insists that he does not want to work with all the added stresses since he has a young grandson he watches. Uncle Junior then adds "Why are you listening to him for? He never had the makings of a varsity athlete!"

Feech La Manna tells a local gardener, Sal Vitro, who has been cutting grass in a particular neighborhood for several years, that his nephew E. Gary La Manna reserves the rights to mow the lawn in this neighborhood. When Sal Vitro tells him to "fuck off", Feech badly injures him. Paulie Walnuts then learns from his Aunt Mary, who is a loyal customer to Sal, that Sal will not be gardening the area anymore because he was beat up. Paulie tries to help Sal win back his neighborhood but Feech refuses to compromise and throws Paulie out of his bakery. Paulie then pays a visit to Gary La Manna, who is pruning a tree high up with support from his brother. Paulie asks Gary to give back his area to Vitro, and Gary refuses, causing Paulie to throw something at his brother, who as a result pulls La Manna down from the tree. Paulie confiscates Gary's lawn mower, and tells Gary that he must pay Sal's medical bills. Paulie and Feech have a sit-down with Tony, who rules out that Sal and Gary both keep half of their areas. When Sal hears this, he is disappointed, especially when told he will have to work for free at the homes of made men.

During Sunday dinner at Uncle Junior's, which Janice claims to have made despite having purchased many of dinner's courses from Nuovo Vesuvio's takeout menu, Uncle Junior once again says the phrase Tony had regretted—that he doesn't have the makings of a varsity athlete. When Barbara and her family arrives she asks her brother about some season tickets of the NFL, until Junior intervenes by saying one more time that "He never had the makings of a varsity athlete". Angered, Tony tells A.J. they are leaving and they both then leave.

When Tony once again tries to have a sit-down with Johnny to resolve the New York issue, Christopher intrudes. Johnny then reminds him that he was once a driver and that he should probably still be a driver. On the drive from the meeting, suggests that Chris keep his ears open and mouth shut for the future. Meeting in a lot in Coney Island the following night, Tony and Johnny try to resolve the issue by using Tony's oligarchy plan. Johnny, however, immediately becomes offended.

Meanwhile Uncle Junior evades Tommy's supervision when Tommy falls asleep, and Junior wanders from his house in his bathrobe. Junior drives to Bloomfield Avenue where his brother Johnny once had a Soprano family hangout, but in its place is now a church, and after being denied entry, leaves his car behind. While he is sitting on a park bench, a homeless woman who offers to give him a blowjob but refuses saying that he has to prioritize finding his car. He is eventually discovered by police walking across a Newark bridge, and he is driven home. When Janice tells Tony this and states she is concernd he might have alzheimers, he claims not to care, due to resentment over the "varsity athlete" comments. Tony and Janice then begin to fight until Tony reminds her of people she has tried to help in the past but failed.

After running into Junior's neurologist on the golf course, Tony realizes that Junior's comments may have been because of his condition. Tony visits Junior to reconcile, and recommends that he take his medication to help with his memory loss. When Tony asks Junior if he loves him, Junior doesn't answer, but weeps quietly.

Trivia

- To date, this is the only episode where Edie Falco does not appear.

- Junior insults Tony by saying "he will never be a varsity athlete" - this was a repetition of comments that Junior made about Tony in the past, as discussed in Tony's therapy in the Pilot.

- The episode marks the return of Tony's sister, Barbara, who was absent during Season 4. The role was previously played by Nicole Burdette, now replaced with actress Danielle Di Vecchio.

- A bartender is reading a New York Post before Lorraine Calluzzo and Jason Evanina walk in and are promptly beaten by Phil Leotardo and Joey Peeps. Calluzzo represents New York Post entertainment journalist Linda Stasi, who gave season four bad reviews, wanting more deaths in the show.

"All Happy Families"

"All Happy Families..." is the 56th episode of the HBO original series, The Sopranos. It was the 4th episode for the show's fifth season. The episode was written by Toni Kalem and was directed by Rodrigo Garcia. It originally aired on March 28, 2004.

Guest Starring

- Frankie Valli as Rusty Millio
- Ray Abruzzo as Little Carmine
- David Strathairn as Robert Wegler
- David Lee Roth as Himself
- Lawrence Taylor as Himself
- Frank Vincent as Phil Leotardo
- Robert Loggia as Feech La Manna
- Chris Caldovino as Billy Leotardo
- Joe Maruzzo as Joe Peeps
- Joe Santos as Angelo Garepe
- Patti D'Arbanville as Lorraine Calluzzo
- John Pleshette as Dr. Ira Fried

Synopsis

The battle between Johnny Sack and Little Carmine over payments has led to the death of Lorraine Calluzzo and her boyfriend/strongman, Jason Evanima. With Phil Leotardo standing guard, , Billy Leotardo and Joe Peeps shoot them to death. When Little Carmine learns of the hit, Angelo Garepe advocates restraint; but another associate, Rusty Millio, disagrees, wanting to steamroll Johnny Sack and predicting that the guys on the street will, in the end, thank them for it.

Meanwhile, Anthony Jr. is having a difficult time in school and is being extremely disagreeable to his mother because he resents his parents' separation. At a parent-teacher conference, Mr. Wegler (AJ's guidance counseler) advises that AJ work on his SAT scores and to do better with his classwork. A.J. is sent back to class with that advice, and Mr. Wegler tries to speak privately with his parents about his academic records. Carmela feels the separation is partially to blame for AJ's poor GPA, but agrees that A.J. should be devoting more time to academics. After they leave the office, the secretary informs Mr. Wegler that two girls were killed in a car accident coming to school that morning. A.J., still in the office talking to a friend, is shocked.

Tony then buys AJ a new Nisson Xterra to cheer him up, but Carmela scoffs at thinks A.J. does not deserve such a gift and it rob him of whatever little amount of motivation he has to do well in school. A.J. talks back to Carmela but then Tony tells A.J. that the car stays in the garage until his grades are up. The following day, A.J. asks his mother if he can attend a concert in New York City with a few friends. Carmela eventually agrees but the stipulation is that he has to go to Meadow's apartment after the concert, instead of to a hotel room with friends, and be back at home by 10am the following morning. A.J. agrees and continues to look at his car manual.

On the night of the concert, A.J. calls Meadow to tell her that he will not be coming to her apartment afterward and then arrives at hotel with his friends where they get high and drunk. The next morning, A.J. and his friend Matt are literally glued to the floor and A.J.'s eyebrows have been shaved off, waking when Carmela calls AJ's cel. Worried, Carmela is about to send Tony after him but. A.J. arrives home, running upstairs and cursing. Tony comes over and his son makes up an alibi to explain why he has no eyebrows and why he is so late. Tony believes him and Carmela then suggests that A.J. go live with Tony at Livia's house. After receiving a phone call from Mr. Wegler, Carmela decides to go out to dinner to discuss her son. The discussion, however, quickly turns to her social life and marriage.

Tony hears the news of Lorraine Calluzo's murder advises his associates not to get involved in the New York feud. Feech La Manna then asks if he can run the card game once again—the same one Tony once knocked off in order to get ahead in the crew faster--and Tony considers the offer since it is now run by Uncle Junior's crew. At the card game, Feech La Manna continues reminiscing and Tony gets frustrated. Using Carmela's suggestion, Tony makes an obviously unfunny joke to the card players to see if they laugh. The only person not laughing is Feech, which means that the other associates are scared and have to laugh because of his rank in the organization.

When Feech carjacks a wedding from one of Tony's close friends, Tony reluctantly decides that Feech must go. Christopher and Benny Fazio go to Feech's house and ask him if they can hide a set of flat screen televisions. Feech recommends that they place them in his garage, but charges them a TV for the service. The following day, Feech's parole officer pays him a visit, and asks Feech to show him his garage. For violating his parole by receiving stolen mechandise, Feech is immediately returned to prison on a bus.

Hits

- Lorraine Calluzzo: shot by Billy Leotardo on orders by Johnny Sack
- Jason Evanina: shot by Joe Peeps for being an associate with Lorraine

Trivia

- The episode's script was written by Toni Kalem, who also plays Angie Bonpensiero on the series.

- The character of Dr. Ira Fried was recast in this episode with actor John Pleshette. The role was previously played by Lewis J. Stadlen.

- This is the first time we see Frankie Valli portraying Lupertazzi capo Rusty Milio. Valli was mentioned before in the season 4 episode "Christopher".

"Irregular Around the Margins"

"Irregular Around the Margins" is the 57th episode of the HBO original series, The Sopranos. It was the 5th episode for the show's fifth season. The episode was written by Robin Green and Mitchell Burgess and was directed by Allen Coulter. It originally aired on April 4, 2004.

Guest Starring

- Jerry Adler as Hesh Rabkin
- Joseph R. Gannascoli as Vito Spatafore
- Lola Glaudini as Agent Deborah Ciccerone-Waldrup
- Karen Young as Agent Sanseverino
- Dan Grimaldi as Patsy Parisi
- Frank Vincent as Phil Leotardo
- Max Casella as Benny Fazio
- Frank Pellegrino as Chief Frank Cubitoso
- Robert Funaro as Eugene Pontecorvo
- Will Janowitz as Finn De Trolio
- Tony Siragusa as Frankie Cortese
- Anthony Ribustello as Dante Greco
- Duke Valenti as Corky DiGioia

Synopsis

Tony has been spending a lot of time at the Crazy Horse, which means he has also been seeing quite a bit of Adriana. One evening where Christopher is out of town on business, the they bond by talking and doing drugs, and drinking over a game of darts. At one point in the dart game, Adriana drops some of them and bends down to pick them up. When Tony helps her up, they share a moment fraught with sexual tension that is broken by the arrival of Phil Leotardo and Joe Peeps.

Back in therapy later that week, Tony tells Dr. Melfi that Adriana is the kind of woman with whom he could start a whole new family, despite knowing that developing such feelings puts him on very dangerous grounds in terms of his relationships with his children, Carmela, and Christopher. Dr. Melfi commends Tony for this psychological "milestone" – thinking before acting about the consequences for his life and for those he loves.

Adriana, meanwhile, is being pressured by the FBI to get even closer to Tony. One night, Tony and Adriana decide to drive to Dover to get some cocaine, Tony swerves to avoid an animal in the road and flips his SUV. Adriana took the worst of the crash, bearing several bruises, but suffered no serious injuries. Word spreads, however, that the reason for the accident was because Adriana was performing oral sex on Tony while he was driving. Christopher hears about the accident when he returns to New Jersey with and hurries back home.

When he goes to Satriale's, he sees Vito and some other wiseguys laughing over the idea that Adriana was giving Tony head so he crashed the car. Christopher goes into a rage and throws food at Vito, who outranks him. Later, he angrily confronts Adriana at home. When he assaults her and chokes her, she admits that she and Tony were going to see her drug dealer, but inisists that nothing happened between them. Christopher beats her anyway and throws her out of their home, then falling off the wagon to drink.

Christopher later shows up drunk at the Bada Bing in search of Tony. He empties his clip into Tony's SUV in the parking lot and enters the bar. Tony's crew subdue him and take him out to an abandoned road where Tony prepares to execute his nephew. Unwilling to believe his uncle, Christopher waits for Tony to shoot him. Tony B. intercedes with a plan to convince Christopher of the truth—that Adriana wasn't giving Tony head.

Christopher and the two Tonys see the doctor who treated Adriana on the night of the accident, and Blundetto is able to convince the doctor to affirm that Adriana was wearing her seatbelt during the accident and could not have been physically involved with Tony. Christopher has been placated, but he is still upset. Everyone else thinks that the false story is true, but Tony asks him why he cares what people think since he knows the truth. Christopher answers that he does not want to look like "Joe Jerkoff."

With this resolved, Tony manages to convince Carmela that nothing happened between Adriana and him, then asks her for help, only for Carmela to complain that she has to bail him out. In a show of solidarity, Tony, Carmela, Christopher, Adriana, Tony B., and Quintina Blundetto arrive at Vesuvio's for all of Tony's crew to see. Vito approaches them and shakes Christopher's hand, wishing him a nice evening.

First Appearances

- Frankie Cortese: Associate in the Soprano crew.
- Dante Greco: Associate in the Aprile crew.

"Sentimental Education"

"Sentimental Education" is the 58th episode of the HBO original series, The Sopranos. It was the 6th episode for the show's fifth season. The episode was written by Matthew Weiner and was directed by Peter Bogdanovich. It originally aired on April 12, 2004.

Guest Starring

- David Strathairn as Robert Wegler
- Paul Schulze as Father Phil Intintola
- Dan Grimaldi as Patsy Parisi
- Joseph R. Gannascoli as Vito Spatafore
- Robert Funaro as Eugene Pontecorvo
- Alison Bartlett as Gwen MacIntyre
- Danielle Di Vecchio as Barbara Soprano Giglione
- Ed Vassalo as Tom Giglione
- Sharon Angela as Rosalie Aprile
- Tom Alderdge as Hugh De Angelis
- Arthur Nascarella as Carlo Gervasi

Synopsis

While at work picking up dirty linen, Tony B's truck is stolen. When he gets back to the laundry, his boss, Sungyon Kim, is convinced Tony B. is somehow responsible for the theft. "Believe me," he says, "I no forget you professional criminal."

Tony B., however, is doing his best to live a strictly civilian lifestyle. With the encouragement of girlfriend Gwen MacIntyre, he's earnestly and doggedly studying for the massage therapist license exam, and eventually Mr. Kim comes to appreciate as such and calls him into his office. He makes an offer to finance a massage studio, run by his daughter and Tony B. "You pass test," he tells Tony B, "then you, me, my daughter make the big success journey."

Meanwhile, A.J. is on the path to failing English, so Carmela visits Mr. Wegler. In addition to discussing A.J., Mr. Bob Wegler, invites Carmela to dinner. Afterwards, they go to his place where, for the first time in twenty years, Carmela has sex with a man who isn't Tony Soprano. Later, and glowing from the evening, Carmela comes home and sneaks past A.J., who's moved back following a physical fight with his father.

Tony B. soon passes his exam and spends his time off renovating the storefront that will become the massage studio. Then one night when he is out walking with his girlfriend, a car zooms past them and a small bag is tossed out its window, containing plastic bindles and thousands of dollars. Gwen convinces Tony B. to throw away the drugs and put the money into the business.

Carmela continues to enjoy seeing Bob and Father Intintola's disapproval, she has no intention of ending it. But one night Bob unexpectedly announces that they should "take a time out." Earlier, had strong-armed A.J.'s English teacher into raising his grade on a term paper and now fears Carmela is a "user" who slept with him to get him to do it. Carmela is devastated. Later she tells her father that because she was once married Tony Soprano, her motives will always be questioned.

Tony B. soon blows his windfall on gambling, clothes for himself and toys for his kids. Then, while painting the walls of the massage studio which he is renovating entirely by himself, he gets into an argument with Gwen on the phone. Immediately after, Kim shows up and Tony B. demands "You fuckin' stroll in?" he screams, "I'm over here bustin' my fuckin' ass!" Then Tony B. punches Kim in the face and beats him with a two-by-four. Soon after, he meets Tony S. at Vesuvio and then says to his cousin, "You mentioned you might need someone to run the swag airbags."

"In Camelot"

"In Camelot" is the 59th episode of the HBO original series, The Sopranos. It was the 7th episode for the show's fifth season. The episode was written by Terence Winter and was directed by Steve Buscemi. It originally aired on April 19, 2004.

Guest Starring

- Frank Vincent as Phil Leotardo
- Polly Bergen as Fran Feltstein
- Tim Daly as J.T. Dolan
- Joseph R. Gannascoli as Vito Spatafore
- Joseph Siravo as Johnny Boy Soprano
- Max Casella as Benny Fazio
- Paul Schulze as Father Phil Intintola
- Jerry Adler as Hesh
- Leslie Bega as Valentina la Paz
- Chris Caldovino as Billy Leotardo
- Carl Caportorto as Little Paulie Germani
- Danielle Di Vecchio as Barbara Soprano Giglione
- Arthur Nascarella as Carlo Gervasi

Synopsis

While attending his Aunt Concetta's funeral, Tony sees an elderly lady at his parents' graves. He asks if she was a friend of his mother, but he soon discovers that she is Fran Felstein, his father's longtime goomara. Tony ends up spending quite a bit of time with her and discovers, among other things, that his childhood dog, Tippy, was given to Fran's family when Tony's mother made his father give it away. Fran also tells Tony about all the times she resisted advances made to her by Junior and the one-time fling she had with President Kennedy.

According to Fran, Phil Leotardo and Hesh cheated her out of an investment Tony's father had left for her. Tony tries to collect the money for her, but when Phil avoids him, they end up in a car chase end Phil crashes his car.

Meanwhile, Christopher spends a lot of time with J.T. Dolan, a friend he met in rehab, so they can support eachother and help eachother stay clean. Christopher introduces Dolan to high stakes poker, either oblivious or indifferent as to the potential for his friend to end up with a gambling addiction in place of his former drug addiction. After Dolan runs up $57,000 in debt and starts missing payments, Christopher and Little Paulie give him a beating. J.T. loses some writing assignments, further compounding his problems. He eventually turns back to heroin, so Christopher helps direct him back to rehab after taking his car and making plans to collect more money later.

Tony's relationship with Fran begins to take on a less-rosy hue as he realizes his father was often with her when he should have been with his family, including one night when his mother was hospitalized after a miscarriage and Tony was forced to lie for his father. When he discusses these revelations with Dr. Melfi, she suggests he could have more sympathy for his mother. Tony, however, responds by reminding Dr. Melfi that she made his father give away Tippy.

As the episode closes, Tony is telling his buddies at the Bada Bing an exaggerated accounts of Fran's involvement with JFK.

First Appearances

- JT Dolan: Christopher's Alcoholics Anonymous friend who is also a screenwriter.

Hits

- Aunt Concetta: died of a heart attack while watching Meet the Press
- Vincent Patronella: a friend of Uncle Junior's
- Little boy: died in a jacuzzi; Uncle Junior and Bobby attend his funeral
- Uncle Zio: died of natural causes; fifteen days after the death of his wife, Concetta

Trivia

- Fran Felstein claimed to have an affair with President John F. Kennedy, whose period in history was known as Camelot.

- The racetrack owned by Johnny Boy, Hesh and Phil Leotardo was named the Camelot Race Track.

- The song played during the end credits is "Melancholy Serenade", the theme from The Jackie Gleason Show which was composed by Gleason.

"Marco Polo"

"Marco Polo" is the 60th episode of the HBO original series, The Sopranos. It was the 8th episode for the show's fifth season. The episode was written by Michael Imperioli and was directed by John Patterson. It originally aired on April 25, 2004.

Guest Starring

- Toni Kalem as Angie Bonpensiero
- Frank Vincent as Phil Leotardo
- Joe Santos as Angelo Garepe
- Ray Abruzzo as Little Carmine
- Paul Schulze as Father Phil Intintola
- Allison Bartlett as Gwen McIntyre
- Joe Maruzzo as Joe Peeps
- Suzanne Shepherd as Mary De Angelis
- Tom Alderidge as Hugh De Angelis
- Chris Caldovino as Billy Leotardo

Synopsis

The conflict in New York escalates when Little Carmine's party boat gets sunk. Tony still diligently attempts to keep his crew out of the hostilities, meeting with Johnny Sack and agreeing to have

Phil's car fixed even though it was damaged because Phil owed money that Tony was trying to collect on behalf of the payee.

Carmine's crew begins making approaches to Tony B. through his old prison buddy, Angelo Garepe, approaching him along with Rusty Millio to offer him a freelance job. They want him to kill Johnny Sack's associate Joe Peeps in retaliation for the hit on Lorraine Calluzzo. Tony B. turns them down, but he shortly thereafter comes to grips with the fact that he wants more than he's given within Tony's crew, and isn't moving up very quickly.

Meanwhile, Carmela plans a 75th birthday party for her father. After Uncle Junior ruins the surprise, the old man himself gets involved with planning the event. When he hears Tony is not invited, he gets agitated and demands the "man of the house" attend. When Tony arrives at the party, Carmela's mother Mary is humiliated at his behavior and presentation, apologizing on behalf of the Sopranos to her more high falutin friends. Hugh, however, is thrilled to see Tony. When Tony gives Hugh a Beretta rifle, one of Mary's friends remarks loudly that the best Berettas never leave Italy. As her parents leave, Carmela expresses her disappointment at her mother for her behavior and comments.

After most of the guests depart, Artie leads the younger guests in a game of Marco Polo. During the game, Tony and AJ throw Carmela in the pool, where she is immediately made "it" by Artie. Later, Tony and Carmela find themselves alone in the pool. A few kisses then lead to them spending the night together.

The evening at the Sopranos' house seemed to irritate Tony B., particularly at the way Carmela gave him orders to help her at the party. His sons were dissatisfied returning to their own home after they had so much fun at the Sopranos'. After thinking everything over, Tony B. calls Rusty and agrees to do the hit. He finds Joe Peeps outside a house of ill repute in his car and shoots him and his female companion, injuring his foot when the vehicle rolls over it. He then limps back to his own car to make his getaway.

Hits

- Joe Peeps: shot by Tony Blundetto on Little Carmine's orders
- Heather: prostitute with Joe Peeps; shot by Tony Blundetto

Trivia

- The movie Junior is watching when Bobby enters is the Fellini film La Dolce Vita. Junior references the opening scene with the statue of Jesus being flown over Rome by helicopter with his comment that "you could tell it was a dummy!"

"Unidentified Black Males"

"Unidentified Black Males" is the 61st episode of the HBO original series, The Sopranos. It was the 9th episode for the show's fifth season. The episode was written by Matthew Weiner and Terence Winter and was directed by Tim Van Patten. It originally aired on May 2, 2004.

Guest Starring

- Frank Vincent as Phil Leotardo
- Frankie Valli as Rusty Millio
- Joseph R. Gannascoli as Vito Spatafore
- Dan Grimaldi as Patsy Parisi
- Max Casella as Benny Fazio
- Karen Young as Agent Sanseverino
- Joe Santos as Angelo Garepe
- Ray Abruzzo as Little Carmine
- Robert Funaro as Eugene Pontecorvo
- Chris Caldovino as Billy Leotardo
- Will Janowitz as Finn De Trolio
- Carl Capotorto as Little Paulie Germani
- Arthur Nascarella as Carlo Gervasi

Synopsis

While playing golf with Johnny Sack, Tony learns that all that is known about the man who killed Joey Peeps is that he walked with a limp. This causes Tony to nearly pass out with one of his panic attacks as he realizes that Tony B has an injured foot. After hearing his cousin's unconvincing denials, Tony tells Sack that he and his cousin spent the evening looking for Tony B's estranged daughter. Trying to prevent Tony B. from acting on his own again, Tony gives his cousin more responsibilities in the business and promises to help try to get Tony B. to be official mafioso.

Later, Tony gets Meadow's boyfriend Finn a job working at a construction site and on the job, Finn gets to meet a lot of men in the Soprano crime family. After witnessing a violent encounter between Eugene and Little Paulie, Finn feels uneasy and becomes more nervous when he observes Vito performing oral sex on a security guard one morning before work. Later in the day, Vito invites Finn to a Yankees game, and intimidates him into agreeing. Now scared as to Vito's motives, Finn decides to leave the New Jersey area and after a heated disagreement with Meadow, they agree to get married.

In a session with Dr. Melfi, Tony admits the truth about what he was doing the night Tony Blundetto got arrested. His story about being beaten up by black guys was a lie to cover up a panic attack he suffered after arguing with his mother Livia.

Carmela is still trying to get a divorce, but yet another lawyer has declined to take her case because of who she is married to. She becomes tearful as she gazes out the window of her home and seeing Tony on a float in the backyard pool as Meadow is on the phone to her sharing the news of her engagement to Finn.

Trivia

- The title referring to "unidentified black males" is referenced several times in the episode:

- Tony blames the black males for his mugging the night Tony B. was arrested.

- Tony B. blames black gang members for his foot injury.

- When Eugene smashes a bottle on Little Paulie's head, they agree to blame it on some unidentified black men.

- When Meadow tells Finn of Jackie Jr.'s death, she repeats the false story that he was killed by black drug dealers.

- Joe Gannascoli came up with the idea of Vito being a gay mobster after reading about a member of the Gambino crime family who was gay and allowed to live for the sake of being a good earner.

"Cold Cuts"

"Cold Cuts" is the 62nd episode of the HBO original series, The Sopranos. It was the 10th episode for the show's fifth season. The episode was written by Robin Green & Mitchell Burgess and was directed by Mike Figgis. It originally aired on May 9, 2004.

Guest Starring

- Frank Vincent as Phil Leotardo
- David Strathairn as Robert Wegler
- Joseph R. Gannascoli as Vito Spatafore
- Dan Grimaldi as Patsy Parisi
- Max Casella as Benny Fazio
- Frank Albanese as Uncle Pat Blundetto
- Sharon Angela as Rosalie Aprile
- Chris Caldovino as Billy Leotardo
- Arthur Nascarella as Carlo Gervasi

Synopsis

Tony learns that Johnny Sack has taken the entirety of a load of stolen Vespas that were supposed to be received by Carlo Gervasi's crew and split between the two families. When he confronts Sack, he mobster denies the possession of the Vespas, and makes a veiled, but not that veiled reference to Tony's continued denial that his cousin Tony Blundetto was involved in the murder of Joey Peeps.

Later, Tony demands that Bobby "take control" of his wife when Janice makes the news after getting arrested for beating up a parent at a youth soccer game. Bobby gives her an ultimatum to either see a therapist for anger management or else "this thing with us ain't gonna work out."

The "Soprano temper" becomes the focus of Tony's next session with Dr. Melfi. She comments that depression can be a manifestation of rage turned inward.

Tony sends Christopher and Tony B. to Uncle Pat's farm in upstate New York. The farm has been sold and soon will be home to its new owners, so they must locate and move three bodies that have been dumped and buried there in the past. Christopher and Tony B. bond while doing the night work, but once Tony joins them, he and Blundetto fall back into their old routine of picking on Christopher. Christopher doesn't feel that it's so funny, taking personally the jabs aimed at his substance abuse recovery.

Once back in New Jersey, Tony visits the Bada Bing and initiates a discussion of the terrorist threat tied to unexamined cargo containers at the ports. Georgie, however, upon giving his two cents, recieves a beating from Tony that puts him in the hospital. Tony is afterwards sheepish and apologetic, handing Paulie a wad of bills and insisting he make sure Georgie gets "the best".

Paulie then tells Tony that Georgie does not want to see him again and is quitting his job at the Bada Bing.

Tony joins Janice and Bobby for dinner, but is somewhat annoyed when he sees Janice deal calmly with a series of minor setbacks, demonstrating her newfound mastery of the "Soprano temper". He tests the newly docile Janice by harping sarcastically on the topic of her estranged son, Harpo, and asking "what's French-Canadian for I grew up without a mother". Janice eventually explodes and chases Tony around the room with a fork. Smug, Tony leaves.

First Apearances

- Uncle Pat Blundetto: Tony and Tony B.'s uncle who was given an early retirement from the DiMeo crime family. He settled on a farm in Upstate New York where he was often visited by his nephews Christopher, Tony and Tony B.

Trivia

- In the audio commentary, director Mike Figgis points out how the scene where Christopher and Tony Blundetto dig up the skeletal remains of a man Christopher knew (and killed) echoes a scene in Hamlet.

- Steve Buscemi's character Tony Blundetto says he was teased as a youngster and called Ichabod Crane. When Christopher asks who called him that, Tony answers "some very sorry people", suggesting he sought vengeance on them. In Billy Madison, Buscemi's character keeps a list of "people to kill", which included people who had teased him when he was young.

- The final song is the live version of "I'm Not Like Everybody Else" by The Kinks, which is featured on their album To the Bone.

- Tony delivers another beating to the Bada Bing bartender, Georgie Santorelli, on a trivial premise, which had become a feature of each season since the show's inception.

- Though credited, Dominic Chianese, Jamie Lynn DiScala, Robert Iler, Katherine Narducci, and John Ventimiglia do not appear in this episode.

"The Test Dream"

"The Test Dream" is the 63rd episode of the HBO original series, The Sopranos. It was the 11th episode for the show's fifth season. The episode was written by David Chase and Matthew Weiner and was directed by Allen Coulter. It originally aired on Sunday May 16, 2004.

Guest Starring

- John Heard as Vin Makazian
- Al Sapienza as Mikey Palmice
- Vincent Pastore as Big Pussy Bonpensiero
- David Proval as Richie Aprile
- John Fiore as Gigi Cestone
- Joe Pantoliano as Ralph Cifaretto
- Tony Lip as Carmine Lupertazzi
- Leslie Bega as Valentina La Paz
- Kathrine Narducci as Charmaine Bucco
- Joe Santos as Angelo Garepe
- Frank Vincent as Phil Leotardo
- Chris Caldovino as Billy Leotardo
- Richard Portnow as Harold Melvoin
- Joseph Siravo as Johnny Boy Soprano
- Will Janowitz as Finn DeTrolio
- Robert Funaro as Eugene Pontecorvo
- Annabella Sciorra as Gloria Trillo

- Annette Bening as Herself

Synopsis

Tony's girlfriend Valentina's clothing catches fire while she is making eggbeaters for Tony. After Tony spends time with her in the hospital, he drops in on Tony B. Tony can tell something is amiss despite Tony B's assurances otherwise, and his instincts are correct: Tony B had just learned about the death of his jailhouse friend, Angelo.

Angelo had picked up a toy for his grandchild when Phil and Billy Leotardo stopped him, threw him in the trunk of Phil's car and shot him in the head. After Tony checks himself into the Plaza for a little rest and relaxation, Tony hears about the murder and tries to call Tony B., who is unable to come to the phone he is on the way to avenge the murder of his friend.

After ordering an Asian prostitute, Tony goes to sleep and has a dream that lasts for about 20 minutes of the episode. The dream is Tony's most vivid yet, full of imagery, ideas and symbolism that reflects the entire run of the series and with characters both living and dead, including Carmine Lupertazzi, Johnny Boy Soprano, Big Pussy Bonpensiero, Ralph Cifaretto, Mikey Palmice, Detective Vin Makazian (posing as Finn's father), Gigi Cestone, Richie Aprile, Gloria Trillo and Pie-O-My.

Several of the characters in his dream communicate that Tony's job was to kill his cousin to prevent Tony B. from starting a war between Tony's family and Johnny Sack's crew. Tony encounters his old football coach, who criticizes Tony, pointing out how Tony had all the prerequisites to be a leader. When Tony tries to kill his former coach his gun malfunctions, and the coach continues to taunt him until Tony wakes up.

Tony gets a visit from Christopher who informs him that Tony B. indeed went after the Leotardo Brothers. He killed Billy and wounded Phil.

Tony calls Carmela and talks to her as the sun rises. They joke with each other on the phone, and then Tony tells her he had "another" dream about Coach Molinaro and pointed out how the coach gave him his usual advice.

Hits

- Angelo Garepe: murdered by Phil and Billy Leotardo.
- Billy Leotardo: murdered by Tony Blundetto in revenge for the death of Angelo Garepe.

Trivia

- The voice on the end of the phone in the dream sequence is that of David Chase.

- Actress Annette Bening also features in the dream as Finn's mother

- The book that Tony finds in the men's bathroom during his dream is the Valachi Papers written by Peter Maas. It is based on the testimony of the first major informant within the Mafia and first person to confirm the existence of Cosa Nostra.

- Tony reaching behind the toilet and the later reference to the "piece" is a reference to a similar scene with Michael Corleone in The Godfather.

- Mikey Palmice's single line in the car stating he has no opinion is similar to a scene in which Marvin is shot in the car in Pulp Fiction.

- When Tony Blundetto shoots Phil Leotardo in Tony Soprano's dream, he exits the car in the same fashion as Sonny Corleone, during the famous shooting scene in The Godfather. He is also wearing the same sort of suit.

"Long Term Parking"

"Long Term Parking" is the 64th episode of the HBO original series, The Sopranos. It was the 12th episode for the show's fifth season. The episode was written by Terence Winter and was directed by Tim Van Patten. It originally aired on May 23, 2004.

Guest Starring

- Nick Tarabay as Matush
- Homie Doroodian as Kamal
- Frank Vincent as Phil Leotardo
- Frankie Valli as Rusty Millio
- Vinny Vella as Jimmy Petrille
- Joseph R. Gannascoli as Vito Spatafore
- Patty McCormack as Liz La Cerva
- Frank Pellegrino as Bureau Chief Frank Cubitoso
- Karen Young as Agent Sanseverino
- Matt Servitto as Agent Harris
- Leslie Bega as Valentina la Paz
- Chris Caldovino as Billy Leotardo
- Ray Abruzzo as Little Carmine
- Arthur Nascarella as Carlo Gervasi

Synopsis

Because Tony Blundetto shot and killed Billy Leotardo, the Soprano crew is compelled to have a meeting with the New York crew. Tony says he doesn't know where Tony B is, but the New York crew is not satisfied. Sack hints that Christopher could stand in for Tony when he says that another of Tony's cousins could be substituted for Blundetto. Before the meeting ends, Sack tells Tony to either deliver Blundetto or prepare for war.

During their surveillance of Adriana's nightclub, the federal agents Adriana carrying a garbage bag out of the club, which she throws into a dumpster only to retrieve later and place in her car trunk. Through further investigation, they learn that a murder took place in the club that night and Adriana had helped to hide evidence.

Tony, meanwhile, wants to reconcile with his wife. He promises to be faithful, but Carmela asks for more—she wants money so she can begin building a special house on a piece of real estate which she believes is a good investment. Tony agrees and plans to return home. He then visits Valentina and breaks up with her. Still in the hospital from the burn injuries she sustained making egg beaters for Tony, she does not take the breakup very well.

Tony receives a phone call from Tony B. and figures out where he called him from via a tracer on his phone—a business near Uncle Pat's farm in upstate Nw York. Tony agrees to look after

Blundetto's two sons and admits to him the truth about the night Blundetto got arrested many years ago.

The FBI confronts Adriana and threatens her with twenty-five years in prison for obtructing their investigation, but Adriana convinces them to let her talk to Christopher and try to persuade him to enter the witness protection program. Christopher reacts violently to her proposal before seeming to agree. He tells her he is leaving to get some cigarettes but never returns. Tony calls her later and tells her that Christopher tried to commit suicide, and that Silvio is on his way over to take her to the hospital. But Silvio instead drives her into the woods and shoots her twice as she attempts to get away, killing her.

Tony meets with Christopher at the Bing to see how he's doing. He cops to snorting heroin to help him feel better, telling Tony he loved Adriana. Tony loses his composure and gives Christopher a beating.

After word gets to New Jersey that Johnny Sack has become the unquestioned successor to Carmine, Tony meets the new Boss at their usual place by the East River. Tony asks that he be given the chance to kill his cousin Tony B. so that he does not suffer, but Sack says Phil is going to do it "his way". After a cursing at Sack, Tony leaves.

Hits

- Adriana La Cerva: Shot by Silvio
- Gilbert Nieves: stabbed in the abdomen by Matush

Trivia

- Terence Winter won the Emmy for Outstanding Writing for a Drama Series for his work on this episode.

- Christopher's line "The highway's jammed with broken heroes on a last chance power drive" is from Bruce Springsteen's Born to Run.

- Drea de Matteo confirmed in her 2005 audio commentary that the death of Adriana La Cerva was real.

- Steven Van Zandt and Drea De Matteo went to David Chase and asked him to cut out the scene where Christopher tells Tony about Adriana in order to keep the death of Adriana at the hands of Silvio a surprise.

"All Due Respect"

"All Due Respect" is the 65th episode of the HBO original series, The Sopranos. It was the season finale for the show's fifth season. The episode was written by David Chase and Robin Green & Mitchell Burgess and was directed by John Patterson. It originally aired on Sunday June 6, 2004.

Guest Starring

- Frank Vincent as Phil Leotardo
- Jerry Adler as Hesh Rabkin
- Joseph R. Gannascoli as Vito Spatafore
- Robert Funaro as Eugene Pontecorvo
- George Loros as Raymond Curto
- Max Casella as Benny Fazio
- Tony Darrow as Larry Boy Barese
- Tom Aldredge as Hugh De Angelis
- Denise Borino as Ginny Sacrimoni
- Jessica Dunphy as Devin Pillsbury
- David Marguilles as Neil Mink
- Marianne Leone as Joanne Moltisanti
- Arthur Nascarella as Carlo Gervasi
- Vinny Vella as Jimmy Petrille

Synopsis

As New York continues to press violence onto Soprano soldiers, particularly Benny Fazio, and threatening Christopher, Tony knows he must do something about Tony B. At Raymond Curto's birthday dinner, Tony states in a speech that "[they] must deal with this as a family and those of [them] who are not with him...will be dealt with in time". Vito states that he would be willing to die for a good cause, but this situation is doesn't qualify as a good cause. At the pork store, Larry Boy Barese and associates discuss Tony's favoritism towards his cousin and that he would have surrendered anyone else.

Tony seeks out help from Dr. Melfi but as he is unable to tell her the details of what is bother him, she can't be very helpful. Dr. Melfi also becomes annoyed and frustrated because a majority of Tony's life is excluded from the therapy sessions. Tony then asks for the advice of Uncle Junior who is still under house arrest but his short attention span limits his helpfulness as well -- he's more concerned about sending a fruit basket to his lawyer. Tony then visits Paulie and sees the painting of Pie-O-My and himself which was supposedly burned. He immediately takes it down and brings it to a dumpster, pausing at first, and then throwing it away. As Tony Blundetto arrives back at the farm after buying groceries, Tony emerges with a rifle and shoots his cousin in the head, then informing Johnny where Tony B is hiding. When Phil arrives he expects Tony B. to be in the house but is surprised to see nothing but Tony B's body lying on a wood pile. Johnny Sack later calls Tony and tells him that "it didn't solve nuttin'". Tony agrees to meet Johnny the following morning at Johnny's house to settle the families' feud.

Then Tony asks Christopher's help to bury their cousin Tony B. Tony asks Chris if Adriana may have mentioned anything to the FBI about Matthew Bevilaqua and Ralph Cifaretto. Christopher still feels angered and betrayed about it all, but he says that he was careful not talk in front of her about anything that might be construed as information leading to the murders.

A.J. plans a party with a friend and they end up netting $300. When Carmela and Tony learn about his fondness for throwing parties, Carmela reveals that A.J. asked his guidance counselor which colleges would be suitable for studying event planning. Tony experiences some cognitive dissonance about this as he feels that this particular line of work might be "gay", but is happy that his son is interested in something.

The following morning Tony and Johnny meet at John's New Jersey home and Tony offers a percentage of the Bloomfield Avenue casino as an olive branch for John to pass along to Phil. John considers the offer and Tony hopes to continue working with the New York family, but when Tony spots FBI agents coming from the woods, he runs, leaving John behind. The FBI raid the Sacramoni home and arrest John. A few hours later, Tony calls his lawyer to ask what has happened. John has been brought up on charges which were built with the help of Jimmy Petrille, who had flipped years ago. Neil advises Tony to be happy since Tony was not mentioned in the indictment. In the snowy weather, Tony continues to walk the long route home.

Hits

- Tony Blundetto: murdered by Tony Soprano to appease the Lupertazzi family.

Trivia

- Vito prefaces his criticism with "All due respect" when discussing the family's problems with New York with the other captains.

- Silvio tells "All due respect" to Tony before criticizing him for having too much pride. The phrase is intended to be one of reverence, but usually precedes someone in authority being told something they don't want to hear.

- This is the final episode directed by John Patterson. Patterson died in 2005.

- Van Morrison's Glad Tidings plays in the episode and in the end credits.

Season 6

"Members Only"

"Members Only" is the 66th episode of the HBO original series, The Sopranos. It was the first episode for the show's sixth season. The episode was written by Terence Winter and was directed by Tim Van Patten. It originally aired on Sunday March 12, 2006.

Guest Starring

- Jerry Adler as Hesh Rabkin
- Frankie Valli as Rusty Millio
- Robert Funaro as Eugene Pontecorvo
- George Loros as Raymond Curto
- Max Casella as Benny Fazio
- Lenny Venito as Murmur
- Matt Servitto as Agent Dwight Harris
- Karen Young as Agent Robyn Sanseverino
- Lou Martini, Jr. as Anthony Infante
- Denise Borino as Ginny Sacrimoni
- Tom Aldredge as Hugh De Angelis
- Danielle Di Vecchio as Barbara Soprano Giglione
- Arthur Nascarella as Carlo Gervasi
- John Bianco as Gerry Torciano

Synopsis

Over a year has passed from the end of the fifth season: Vito has lost a tremendous amount of weight, A.J. is in college, Janice and Bobby have a baby, questions continue to be asked about Adriana's whereabouts, and Artie Bucco is reuniting with his ex-wife, Charmaine, after years of being divorced. Carmela and Angie Bonpensiero patch up a long quarrel and both show off their new cars: Carmela, a Cayenne and Angie, a Corvette.

Phil Leotardo is now in charge of Johnny Sack's operations while Johnny is in jail. After eating at a Chinese restaurant in Brooklyn, Hesh and his son-in-law are beaten up by Phil's men, and his son-in-law is hit by a car when he tries to run. At the hospital, Hesh asks Tony for help to settle the feud. Phil and Tony also have a disagreement on their cut from their latest building project, and both incidents are discussed in a meeting between the two families, during which Phil is no longer venomous towards Tony and Christopher, and the issues are resolved.

Eugene Pontecorvo has recently come into money. He inherited two million dollars from his aunt, and he and his wife Deanne want to get away from the crime life and move to Florida. Gene goes to Tony with a gift and a request to retire to Florida. Tony tells Eugene he took an oath, and that retiring is not an option. As it turns out, Eugene is cooperating with the FBI, who now increase their pressure on him to produce information, having lost cooperator Raymond Curt. Eugene decides his family will do better with him dead than alive, and hangs himself.

Later, Tony runs into Agent Harris at the pork store and he tells Tony he has been in Pakistan because he was transferred to terrorism.

Meanwhile, Uncle Junior's mental state has markedly deteriorated. He attempts to find money he thinks he buried many years ago in his backyard, and is convinced "Little Pussy" Malanga is out to get him. When Tony shows up to spend time with his uncle, Junior seems particularly confused and paranoid. As Tony begins to make something for Junior to eat, Junior heads upstairs under the auspices of finding his false teeth, and instead gets a gun and shoots Tony in the stomach. Uncle Junior then runs up the stairs and hides in the closet, under the impression that he just shot Little Pussy Malanga, as Tony struggles to call 911.

First Appearances

- Anthony Infante: Ginny Sacramoni's brother who owns an eyewear store.
- Domeneica Baccalieri: Janice and Bobby's 12 month old daughter.
- "Murmur": an associate of Christopher and his AA sponsor first seen at Raymond's funeral.

- Gerry Torciano: associate in the Lupertazzi crime family responsible for Phil Leotardo's business in Brooklyn following his promotion to acting boss.

Hits

- Raymond Curto: stroke
- Teddy Spirodakis: shot in chicken restaurant in Boston by Eugene
- Eugene Pontecorvo: suicide by hanging
- Dick Barone: (off-screen) owner of Barone Sanitation; died of Amyotrophic lateral sclerosis.

Trivia

- The episode's writer Terence Winter won an Emmy for Outstanding Writing in a Drama series at the 58th Annual Primetime Emmy Awards.

- The opening sequence features a montage of the characters is showing what has happened in the past two years.

- Pussy Malanga, the man Uncle Junior was convinced is coming for him and mistakes Tony for is the same mobster Uncle Junior wanted to kill in Artie Bucco's restaurant in the pilot episode.

- Adriana resurfaces in Carmela's dream where the two talk about her new project, and Carmela wakes up very upset.

- Although both characters have interacted before, this is the first time we see Phil calling Vito "cugino mio" ("my cousin").

- Frank Vincent (Phil Leotardo), Joseph Gannascoli (Vito Spatafore), Dan Grimaldi (Patsy Parisi) and Toni Kalem (Angie Bonpensiero) are now billed in the opening credits.

- Part of William Burroughs work "Seven Souls" is read during the opening sequence.

- In the original broadcast of this episode on March 12, 2006, no previews for the next episode were shown in order to keep the aftermath of Tony's shooting a mystery.

- When Eugene shoots Teddy in the chicken restaurant, he fires three shots, which results in 3 blood splatters over the window. On the pull back camera view, when Eugene leaves, there are only two gobs of blood splattered on the window.

"Join the Club"

"Join the Club" is the 67th episode of the HBO original series, The Sopranos. It was the second episode for the show's sixth season. The episode was written by David Chase and was directed by David Nutter. It originally aired on Sunday March 19, 2006.

Guest Starring

- Sheila Kelley as Lee
- Jerry Adler as Hesh Rabkin
- Tony Darrow as "Larry Boy" Barese
- Sharon Angela as Rosalie Aprile
- Maureen Van Zandt as Gabriella Dante
- Will Janowitz as Finn DeTrolio
- Robert Funaro as Eugene Pontecorvo
- Matt Servitto as Agent Harris
- Danielle Di Vecchio as Barbara Soprano Giglione
- Arthur Nascarella as Carlo Gervasi

Synopsis

Tony is still in critical condition two days after the shooting. The attendant physicians in the ICU sedate Tony into an induced coma after he becomes agitated from a dream and attempts to remove his breathing tube. Doctors inform Carmela that Tony suffers from blood poisoning and many other complications, and encourage Carmela and others to talk to him and play him music in the hopes of a recovery. However, they also warn his family members that even if he makes it, there are prospects of brain damage. Carmela asks the doctor if Tony is "aware that he's dying."

A vigil of Tony's family members and business associates have assembled in the ICU and Carmela, Christopher, and Meadow sleep in the hospital.

Meanwhile, Uncle Junior is in custody and is being interrogated about the shooting but confused, he is openly hostile and does not remember that he has a new lawyer. He also insists that Tony's wound must have been self-inflicted because Tony suffers from depression.

Christopher, Paulie, and Vito vie for small opportunities to assist Tony's family, such as sending presents to Tony's room and arguing over who gets to give A.J. a ride home.

During the wake of the late soldier Eugene Pontecorvo, Silvio assumes Tony's responsibilities as family boss. At the impromptu meeting the crew also talks about their feelings about Junior—some are furious at Junior, and others are suspicious of why Bobby—traditionally Junior's caretaker—was not in the house that night. Also, Vito makes a bid to take over Eugene's sportsbook responsibilities, and later, implies to Janice that perhaps Eugene had been a homosexual who had no one to talk to.

Meanwhile, A.J. avoids Tony's room, neglecting his familial and school responsibilities. He talks to a reporter at the hospital, but curses the ones camped outside the Soprano home; he forgets to bring requested items to the hospital to assist in Tony's recovery, a questionable stomach flu excuses him from being at the hospital one night, and develops a preoccupation with hybrid cars. This worries Carmela, who voices her concerns to Rosalie Aprile. With the death of her own wayward son Jackie Aprile, Jr. fresh in both their minds, Rosalie advises Carmela to engage in stricter parenting with A.J.; however, Carmela fears that A.J.'s deep esteem for his father is the source of his aloofness.

A.J. comes clean to Meadow, admitting that he is embarrassed and angry , particularly at Uncle Junior, whom he calls a "mummy." A.J. finally gives in to his family's wishes to talk to his comatose father. Once the two are alone A.J. goes on and on about hybrid cars, and then vows to avenge Tony's death by killing Uncle Junior. Immediately afterwards, tells Carmela that he failed out of junior college.

Tony has a long dream-like, surreal experience while he is in a coma. He is a precision optical salesman on a business trip, but with a standard American accent instead of his strong Jersey one. In the dream, Tony is at a bar one night. The next morning he goes to a convention, and as he is asked for ID at the door, he realizes that he has someone else's wallet and briefcase. He assumes that he must have unintentionally swapped them with someone else's the previous evening at the bar. After talking to his wife (whose voice is not Carmela's), he realizes that he looks kind of like "Kevin Finnerty", the man whose wallet he now possesses. Tony then checks into a different hotel under Finnerty's name. The next morning he goes out to take the elevator down, but eventually ends up taking the stairs after loitering for some time in front of the bank of elevators. As he is going down the stairs, he slips and falls. In the emergency room, the doctor tells him that aside from having a minor concussion, his CT scan shows that he has the early stages of Alzheimer's disease. When the doctor leaves him at his bed, Tony is seen saying "I'm lost" to himself. After he gets back to his hotel, Tony picks up the phone, but hangs up before even dialing. Although described as a dream by many viewers, the show's creator and writer of the episode has suggested that the experience is not a dream, at least not in the same sense as prior dreams depicted in other episodes of the series.

Trivia

- The exterior of the hosptial is actually Fenster Hall of NJIT

- Lee, the woman at the bar, is curious how Tony made the jump from selling patio furniture to precision optics.

- The credits do not mention the actress (or actresses) playing the voice of Tony's wife in his dream, though the writers have stated the voice is not intended to be anyone else previously featured on the series.

- In the hotel Tony checks in to, under Finnerty's name, he is given a room on the 7th floor. This may be a reference to the seven terraces of Purgatory in Dante's Purgatorio. When Tony falls in the stairwell he lands on the 5th floor. This may allude to the Fifth concentric ring of hell in the Inferno: Avarice or Greed.

"Mayham"

"Mayham" is the 68th episode of the HBO original series, The Sopranos. It was the third episode for the show's sixth season. The episode was written by Matthew Weiner and was directed by Jack Bender. It originally aired on Sunday March 26, 2006.

Guest Starring

- Timothy Daly as J.T. Dolan
- Steve Buscemi as Man
- Paul Schulze as Father Phil Intintola
- Lenny Venito as Murmur
- Max Casella as Benny Fazio
- Elizabeth Bracco as Marie Spatafore
- Carl Capotorto as Little Paulie Germani
- Tony Darrow as Larry Boy Barese
- Maureen Van Zandt as Gabriella Dante
- Danielle Di Vecchio as Barbara Soprano Giglione
- Ed Vassalo as Tom Giglione
- Tom Aldredge as Hugh De Angelis
- Suzanne Shepherd as Mary De Angelis
- Bill Kurtis as Himself

Synopsis

Acting on a tip from Vito, Paulie and a member of his crew attempt to rob what they were told would be an empty apartment full of Colombian drug money. The apartment, however, is far from empty, but this proves to be a minor setback: after getting rid of the superintendent, and two drug dealers, they collect over a million dollars. During the struggle with the assailants, Paulie is kicked in the groin, and later seeks medical attention to deal with the pain.

Back at the hospital, Christopher and Bobby talk to A.J. about his attempt to buy a gun. They tell him they would want to do the same thing, but that Tony would not want him involved and it's not ok for him to kill his great uncle. A.J. afterwards accuses Carmela of putting the two up to the talk, in which he felt he was talked down to, though she has no idea what he's taling about.

Tony, still in the hospital, and still in a dreamlike state, has another experience with Kevin Finnerty. In it, he receives a summons addressed to Kevin Finnerty. He's beginning to question his actual identity. He seeks answers from a bartender and monks, but does not get the information he wants.

Meanwhile, there are rumbles of unhappiness about Silvio's performance as acting boss. When he makes rulings on how Bobby and Vito are to share Eugene's former revenue, and on the cut to be given to Carmela on behalf of Tony from Paulie and

Vito's score, none of the parties involved like his decisions. Paulie and Vito delay giving the money to Carmela, since they do not want to give it up in the event Tony does not recover. Vito openly questions what is to happen if "God forbid" Tony does not make it, and covertly starts a campaign to position himself as a new leader.

Silvio and Paulie manage to flout hospital orders that only family is allowed in Tony's room, and sneak in to see him. When they reach his room, Silvia stands quietly at the doorway staring at his boss before walking over and taking his hand. Exclaims "he looks terrible" as he enters the room, and after being left alone with Tony as Meadow goes to meet Finn's arrival, Paulie delivers a vulgarity-infused diatribe regarding the current state of the crew, including the details of his groin injury and his big score. Tony's heart rate then escalates and he goes into cardiac arrest.

Paulie's voice penetrates through layers of consciousness into Tony's dreamstate, manifested as sounds from the neighboring room in his hotel. Tony tries to ignore the sounds while he gets directions via phone to the Finnerty family reunion, and when he arrives, a man who looks just like his cousin Tony Blundetto is tells him everyone inside is expecting him. The man tries to get Tony to enter the house, telling him that everyone is there and waiting for him, and soon he will be home, but also makes sure Tony understands that in order to enter, he must "let go" and leave all his belongings at the steps. With the figure of someone similar to his mother standing by the doorway in front of him, and the faint voice of a little girl (in reality his daughter's) pleading with him not to go, Tony/Kevin chooses not to enter the house. In the hospital, Tony wakes up from his coma.

Later, heavily sedated and still largely unable to talk, Tony sits in a chair at the foot of his bed and listens to Christopher tell him of his next attempt at breaking into the movie biz.

Meanwhile, succumbing to the pressures of being acting boss, Silvio's asthma begins to bother him and he too ends up at the hospital.

Hits

- Building Superintendent: shot by Colombian #1
- Colombian #1: shot by Cary De Bartolo and then shot by Paulie
- Colombian #2: shot by Cary De Bartolo and then stabbed by Paulie

Trivia

- Although credited as "Man" and not Tony Blundetto, Steve Buscemi shows up in Tony's dream as the host who tries to bring Tony into the afterlife.

- Silvio reveals to his wife that before his death in 1999, acting boss Jackie Aprile suggested that Silvio, not Tony, could be the one to replace him as the head of the family.

"The Fleshy Part of the Thigh"

"The Fleshy Part of the Thigh" is the 69th episode of the HBO original series, The Sopranos. The episode was written by Diane Frolov and Andrew Schneider and was directed by Alan Taylor. It was the 4th episode for the show's sixth season. It originally aired on April 2, 2006.

Guest Starring

- Hal Holbrook as John Schwinn
- Lord Jamar as Da Lux
- Anthony "Treach" Criss as Marvin
- muMs da Schemer as Mop
- Max Casella as Benny Fazio
- Chris Diamantopoulos as Jason Barone
- Paul Schulze as Father Phil Intintola
- Jerry Adler as Hesh Rabkin
- Will Janowitz as Finn De Trolio
- Turk Pipkin as Aaron Arkaway
- Carl Capotorto as Little Paulie Germani
- John "Cha Cha" Ciarcia as Albie Cianflone
- Frances Ensemplare as Marianucci Gualtieri

Synopsis

With his condition improved, Tony has a surgery to close the opening in his stomach. Of course, the insurance company wants to send him home as soon as possible but before leaving, he bonds with two patients on his floor: John Schwinn, a scientist, and Da Lux, a rapper.

Schwinn and Tony talk about the way one's actions have a ripple effect, and how no event can be understood independent from the rest of the world. The scientist has ideas that refute the beliefs of two evangelical visitors to Tony, and he uses the information gained from both sides to debate the other.

Da Lux expresses admiration to Tony, and like Tony, he is hospitalized for gunshot wounds. Unlike Tony, however, he's pretty excited about having been shot, theorizing that this will help his career by giving him "street cred". Bobby proposes an idea to Marvin--one of the other rappers visiting the hospital--to help jumpstart his career with a gunshot wound to his thigh. The rapper agrees, but Bobby instead hits the man on the buttocks.

Meanwhile, Paulie's Aunt Dottie is dying and Paulie visits her. On a particularly memorable visit, she tells him that she's not his aunt; she's actually his mother—since she was a nun, she had to ask her sister raise Paulie as if he was her son. Devastated, Paulie struggles to remain focused at work and questions his own identity confronting the woman who raised him and tells her he will no longer support her financially.

Following Dick Barone's death his son Jason takes over ownership of Barone Sanitation and tries to sell the company without consulting with the Soprano family first. By the time Tony, Paulie and Patsy communicate to him that his best interests will not be served by going through with the sale, Jason discovers he is too far along in the sales process to back out. As it turns out, company trying to buy Barone's routes is associated with Johnny Sack. After a violent encounter between two garbage crews as they tried to work the same route, Tony agrees to Sack's terms and allows the sale to go through, despite not getting the demands he originally stated. He also does not punish Jason for going ahead against his wishes. As he leaves the hospital, Tony again avoids conflict by allowing an EMT worker to keep money Tony originally claimed was taken from his wallet the night his uncle shot him.

Outside the hospital, on his way back home, Tony observes, "from now on, every day is a gift." At the docks Paulie viciously beats Jason and demands a cut from his business, apparently without telling Tony.

Hits

- Aunt Dottie: Paulie's biological mother who dies of natural causes.

Trivia

- The episode references the Hurricane Katrina of 2005. When Jason Barone tells Tony his current situation is unfair, Tony tells him to ask the Hurricane Katrina victims about fair.

- John "Cha Cha" Ciarcia appears in this episode as Albie Cianflone, Phil Leotardo's consigliere. He played one of Billy Batt's crew in Goodfellas. Both Billy Batts and Phil Leotardo are played by Frank Vincent.
- Ray Abruzzo (Carmine "Little Carmine" Lupertazzi, Jr.) is now billed in the opening credits.

- This episode features several real life rappers guest starring as rappers. The rapper/actors have also all appeared in the show Oz.

- The song playing during the end credits is One of These Days by Pink Floyd.

- The exchange between Bob Brewster (the fundamentalist Christian) and Tony references a joke in a comedy routine by Lewis Black on evolution and creationism.

"Mr. And Mrs. John Sacrimoni Request"

"Mr. & Mrs. John Sacrimoni Request..." is the 70th episode of the HBO original series, The Sopranos. The episode was written by Terence Winter and was directed by Steve Buscemi. It was the 5th episode for the show's sixth season. It originally aired on April 9, 2006.

Guest starring

- Frankie Valli as Rusty Millio
- Max Casella as Benny Fazio
- Will Janowitz as Finn De Trolio
- Elizabeth Bracco as Marie Spatafore
- Sharon Angela as Rosalie Aprile
- Maureen Van Zandt as Gabriella Dante
- Denise Borino as Ginny Sacrimoni
- Carl Capotorto as Little Paulie Germani

Synopsis

Johnny Sack is given a six-hour supervised release from prison so that he may go to his daughter's wedding. Despite being in prison, Johnny dominates over the planning of the event, later mentioning that the price tag for the wedding approaches half a million dollars.

Despite having a way sto go in his recovery, Tony is ready to go back to work. He has a new bodyguard, Perry Annunziata, a former bodybuilder that Tony calls "muscles marinara". While on their first trip together, the bodyguard nearly accosts two truck drivers who cut him off and swear at him, but Tony stops him.

Tony's first day back at work mostly consists of playing cards and being waited on by his crew. Phil Leotardo arrives and tells him that Johnny wants Tony to take care of killing Rusty for him. Tony, however, denies the request.

At the wedding, Tony collapses when U.S. Marshals request that he take off his shoes at a security check point. During the reception, once he feels better, he is able to talk to Johnny Sack face-to-face for the first time since he was shot and Johnny was arrested. Johnny asks him again as a personal favor to perform the hit on Rusty, and Tony agrees.

The Marshals break up the send-off for the bride and groom by whisking in to take Johnny away and Johnny to tears up, weeping openly in front of everyone. After he is taken away, members of Tony's crew discuss John's emotional "disgrace", and Phil candidly offers the notion that Johnny is weak and can probably be made to talk by the government. Christopher, however, sides with Phil, directly disagreeing with Tony.

Vito leaves the reception early with complaints of not feeling well, but when he gets home, he tells his wife he needs to make collections. He instead goes out to a gay fetish club, filled with scantily clad men gyrating in leather and chains. Vito dances with a man and offers to buy him a drink, but on the way to the bar, he runs into two of his associates who are there making collections. Vito attempts to play it cool and make a joke, but they call him a "fag" and leave. Vito returns home, gets a gun and checks into a hotel. After a 3 A.M. call to Silvio to "check in" and ask if everything is ok, he makes no further contact with anyone and does not return any calls.

Tony talks to Dr. Melfi about fears that have plagued him since the shooting—that his crew sees him as weak, fragile, and unable to lead. She innocently suggests he do something to let the guys know he is back and healthy, possibly not imagining the way in which Tony will interpret this well-intended advice. He arrives at the pork store and over the guys and seems to try to decide which will pose the greatest physical challenge. He chooses the new bodyguard. In front of his crew, after several attempts to agitate him, Tony punches the brawny olympiad, starting a fight that ends with the Perry bleeding on the floor and Tony walking away unscathed.

However, Tony is not as well as he appears when he saunters away from the scene. He retreats to the bathroom after the altercation and vomits up blood.

Trivia

- In the scene where Ahmed and Mohammed talk to Christopher about the guns, Christopher's stripper is initially in the shot topless. When Christopher's associate calls for him, the stripper has her top back on, and in the following scene, she is once again topless.

- The location of the marriage scene is at "Leonard's" of Great Neck on Northern Boulevard in Long Island, New York.

- Carmela picks up The Star Ledger bearing a picture of Uncle Junior on the cover. This scene can be argued as part of the traditional newspaper sequence which occurs usually in the season premiere of each season. The sixth season premiere however did not use this feature and instead featured an opening montage.

- When dressing for his court appearance, it is stated that Johnny Sack wears a Brioni suit. This could refer to "Dapper Don" John Gotti, who also wore Brioni when going to court.

"Live Free or Die"

"Live Free or Die" is the 71st episode of the HBO original series, The Sopranos. The episode was written by David Chase, Terence Winter, Robin Green, and Mitchell Burgess, and was directed by Tim Van Patten. It was the sixth episode for the show's sixth season. It originally aired on April 16, 2006.

Guest Starring

- Edoardo Ballerini as Corky Caporale
- Max Casella as Benny Fazio
- Tom Alderidge as Hugh De Angelis
- Suzanne Shepherd as Mary De Angelis
- Elizabeth Bracco as Marie Spatafore
- Will Janowitz as Finn DeTrolio
- Lenny Venito as James "Murmur" Zancone
- Maureen Van Zandt as Gabriella Dante
- Arthur Nascarella as Carlo Gervasi

Synopsis

The New York associates who saw Vito in a gay bar have gossiped to seemingly everyone, and the news is on the street. An acquaintance from Yonkers, New York tells Christopher Moltisanti the story, who in turn regales Tony Soprano and his capos with it at the Bada Bing. Paulie Gualtieri and Tony, however, are wary to act on this news, characterizing it as hearsay and conjecture.

Benny Fazio, Dante Greco and Terry Doria drop in on Vito at the beach house of Vito's comare, where he's been laying low. They try to take him to see Tony, but Vito is able to get away. He goes home and after gazing at his children as they sleep, grabs a couple family pictures and a wad of cash, and drives off into the rain. After his car hits a tree branch that has been knocked into the road, Vito is stuck in a small town in New Hampshire.

Vito's mad dash off into the rainy night indicates to Christopher and others that he has something to hide. This is corroborated by Silvio, who after chatting with Marie Spatafore, declares, "I'm around a lot of women. That one ain't getting laid."

The gossip soons spreads further, and Meadow Soprano tells Carmela and her Rosalie Aprile that Finn saw Vito going down on a security guard. Tony drags Finn to the backroom of Satriale's, and urges him to repeat the story to the crew, which convinces even Paulie. The fact that he was "catching" and not "pitching" seems to be an issue with the group. Finn is intimidated by the interrogation and disgusted that the mobsters feel they have to mete out justice because Vito is gay, and he later challenges Meadow's view of her father's business as Italian tradition.

Meadow again questions her family's and friends' values when she sympathises at the law center with an Afghan family whose son was held by police on suspicion of terrorist activity. Her story, instead of garnering sympathy or clucks of disapproval from her family, prompts Tony to ask Christopher if Ahmed and Mohammed, are possibly "al-Qaedas". Christopher tells Tony that they seem too tolerant and Americanised to be terrorists, but is clearly concerned by the suggestion.

Paulie, feeling for some reason that he has been personally betrayed by Vito's sexual proclivities, leads the rallying cry for Vito's blood. Additional chatter makes its way through the group about how Vito's own crew won't follow his orders, and even want to kill him. Tony, admits to Dr. Melfi his ambivalence over whether Vito's homosexuality is really that big an issue, manages to soothe immediate calls for blood while he mulls over what would happen to Vito's family, and to his own income if Vito gets whacked. After Tony implies that he will not go after Vito, Silvio opines that the captains will take clemency as a green light to kick less money up to him. Tony has also reckoned without Phil Leotardo, who arrives to comfort his distraught cousin Marie, both of them now up-to-date on Vito's sexual orientation. Phil ask if Marie can help him locate Vito, under the auspices of to getting him some sort of help.

In his New Hampshire hideaway, Vito makes unsuccesful attempt to locate a cousin, socializes with the townsfolk, and notices a gay couple being welcomed at a local diner. Among the peace and quiet, Vito stops by a picturesque whitewater river, then visits an antique shop where, after admiring one of the items on display, he is commended by the shopkeeper as "a natural" who has "a good eye".

Meanwhile, Carmela discovers that Angie Bonpensiero is doing business with some members of Christopher's crew on the sly, putting money up for street loans and buying stolen car parts. Carmela tries to coax Tony into having the local building inspector allow further work on her spec house, but he forgets about her request, and Carmela is appalled to find that her father Hugh De Angelis has set about selling whatever can be salvaged from their construction site.

Trivia

- The episode's title "Live Free or Die" refers to the New Hampshire state motto

- The scenes filmed for the town of Dartford, New Hampshire were shot in Boonton, New Jersey.

- In the scene with Dr. Melfi, Tony referenced the controversial comments made by Senator Rick Santorum (pronouncing his last name as "Sanatorium") who once claimed the government's allowance of gay marriage would be the first step in a slippery slope leading to tolerance of bestiality.

- The song played during the end credits is "4th of July" by X.

- This is the final episode to be written by the writing team of Robin Green and Mitchell Burgess. Green and Burgess left the series to produce a new project for HBO.

- Sharon Angela (Rosalie Aprile) is now billed in the opening credits.

"Luxury Lounge"

"Luxury Lounge" is the 72nd episode of the HBO original series, The Sopranos. The episode was written by Matthew Weiner and was directed by Danny Leiner. It was the 7th episode for the show's sixth season. It originally aired on April 23, 2006.

Guest Starring

- Edoardo Ballerini as Corky Caporale
- Max Casella as Benny Fazio
- Frankie Valli as Rusty Millio
- Ben Kingsley as Himself
- Lauren Bacall as Herself
- Suzanne Shepherd as Mary De Angelis
- Elizabeth Bracco as Marie Spatafore
- Denise Borino as Ginny Sacrimoni
- Lenny Venito as James "Murmur" Zancone
- Maureen Van Zandt as Gabriella Dante
- Arthur Nascarella as Carlo Gervasi
- Manuela Feris as Martina
- Alicia Lorén as Eden

Synopsis

Under the impression that he is going to be suited up by special tailors from Italy, Rusty Millio and his driver are wacked in the driveway of his home.

At Vesuvio's, Phil Leotardo and Tony Soprano honor two new members: Gerry Torciano and Burt Gervasi. Vito, still missing, is mentioned in a less-than-flattering context, and service is lacking, prompting Phil to tell them about a new restaurant called Da Giovanni. After they finish eating, there is further vitriol regarding Vito, and Chris requests permission of pursuing his dream to make his screenplay into a hollywood film.

Later, Tony finds himself attending the confirmation of Phil's grandson at Da Giovanni's. Vito's wife and children are there, and the kids find themselves the victim of many jokes about their father's sexual orientation. Phil thanks Tony him on Johnny Sack's behalf for taking out Johnny, an act that Tony denies. Phil chooses not to pursue him about it.

Christopher and Little Carmine travel to Los Angeles see about casting Sir Ben Kingsley as the boss in their screenplay: "The Ring meets The Godfather". Unfettered by the shackles of AA and his sponsor, Chris falls off the wagon, drinking, doing drugs, and sleeping with a hooker before calling his sponsor for help.

At the meeting with Kingsley, he is not particarly thrilled about the project, or participating in it, and is more interested in speaking to Lauren Bacall. She enumerates the gifts she will receive for presenting an award that evening, Sir Ben remembers he has a walk-through scheduled in the "luxury lounge" (a room set-up with free gifts handed out to celebrities). Christopher and Carmine come along, with Christopher interested in getting some of the free gifts. Later, he dons a mask and robs Lauren Bacall, scoring her gift bag.

Artie has a new Albanian hostess, Martina, who incites a confrontation between Artie and Benny because she was flirting with the latter at the bar. Artie, as a result, tells her he cannot her get her green card anymore.

Vesuvio's finances are stretched when American Express comes calling to tell Artie that someone has been stealing credit card numbers from his customers, and he will be suspended with them. Later, he finds out that Martina has been in cahoots with Benny in order steal the credit card numbers. Artie, enraged, pays Benny a late night visit, and puts Benny in the hospital before he leaves.

Tony is under the impression that they both are at fault, and tries to get them to reconcile. As part of this program of reconciliation, Benny's parents have their anniversary dinner at Vesuvio, and Artie stops by their table, taking this opportunity to a veiled comment referencing Benny's schemes with Martina.

Benny follows him into the kitchen and manages to put Artie's hand into a boiling pot of tomato sauce.

. When he gets home, Christopher tries to give Tony a piece of the action he got from mugging Lauren Bacall, but Tony is annoyed, thinking Christopher's absence played a part in the Artie-Benny fiasco, stating that if he was around to keep an eye on things it never would have happened.

Tony has dinner at Vesuvio with Carmela and Mary, and Hugh is conspicuosly absent. Tony tries to get Artie to consider the benefits of therapy, doing a bit of armchair diagnosis himself, perhaps to pique Artie's interest in the idea. Tony begins by telling him he feels sorry for himself all the time and that he should stay in the kitchen and not harass his guests with table-side chatter.

Later, Artie is seen in the kitchen and preparing a rabbit dish for two last-minute customers from his father's hand-written cookbook.

Hits

- Rusty Millio: regarded as a threat to the Lupertazzi Family.
- Eddie Pietro: collateral damage from the Millio hit.

"Johnny Cakes"

"Johnny Cakes" is the 73rd episode of the HBO original series, The Sopranos. The episode was written by Diane Frolov and Andrew Schneider and was directed by Tim Van Patten. It was the 8th episode for the show's sixth season. It originally aired on April 30, 2006.

Guest Starring

- Julianna Margulies as Julianna Skiff
- Peter Bogdanovich as Dr. Eliott Kupferberg
- Elizabeth Bracco as Marie Spatafore
- Cameron Boyd as Matt Testa
- John Costelloe as Jim Witowski
- Joseph Leone as Vic Caputo
- Vincent Piazza as Hernan O'Brien
- Artie Pasquale as Burt Gervasi

Synopsis

A.J, seemingly hellbent on sabatoging his future, gives up on work and school almost altogether, hanging out at nightclubs in the city, even selling gifts his father gave him to finance his partying. One day, while fishing with his father, AJ wants to know what they will do about Uncle Junior, but Tony tells AJ that he shouldnt think about punishing his great-uncle. Later, AJ disregards the advice, paying a visit to Uncle Junior in with the intent of killing him, but his will to do so is compromised when Junior asks Aj to take him home. AJ is restrainede by hospital staff and his father manages to get him expediently released form police custody, scolding AJ for thinking he was living a scene in the Godfather.

In New Hampshire, Vito takes on the name "Vince", and the identity of a writer. Despite the amount of time he spends discussing his non-existant authored literature with Jim, he manages to make time to nick someone's cell phone in order to phone his wife. She begs him to come home and to get treatment, and he speaks with his children in a strained, painful conversation.

Vito is missed not only by his family but by his crew, many of whom are interested in finding him and meting out justice for his perceived wrongdoings. Phil, for example, feels strongly that Vito's sexual orientation is his business, but Tony tells him not to worry about it. Phil warns him that he will not turn the other cheek to Vito's homosexuality and marriage to his cousin like he died when Tony Blundetto whacked his brother Billy.

Tony later meets with Julianna, a real estate agent, to see about selling a building that he currently has rented to a poultry store. Tony isn't interested in selling the building but is, however, intrested in Julianna. Persistent, Julianna offers him a second price, which Tony rejects, asking her to dinner despite the fact that she is engaged and he is married. Now it is her turn to reject him, and she declines his offer. Later, she changes her mind, and he changes his. He agrees to sell the building and she makes a move on him. They kiss, but then Tony has second thoughts, stops the makeout session, and leaves the apartment.

After Vito spends an evening with Jim, the latter decides the time is right to hit on the former. Vito, however, is not receptive, and beats Jim up and calls him a bad name that references his sexual orientation. Eventually, Vito has a change of heart, finding himself at the diner, and then going on a romantic picnic with Jim.

Trivia

- The song played during the end credits is "I'm Gonna Move to the Outskirts of Town" by Ray Charles.

"The Ride"

"The Ride" is the 74th episode of the HBO original series, The Sopranos. The episode was written by Terence Winter and was directed by Alan Taylor. It was the 9th episode for the show's sixth season. It originally aired on May 7, 2006.

Guest Starring

- Edoardo Ballerini as Corky Caporale
- Julianna Margulies as Julianna Skiff
- Cara Buono as Kelli Lombardo
- Carl Capotorto as Little Paulie Germani
- Max Casella as Benny Fazio
- Lenny Venito as James "Murmur" Zancone
- Patty McCormack as Liz La Cerva
- Arthur Nascarella as Carlo Gervasi
- Jonathan Del Arco as Father Jose
- Tony Darrow as Larry Boy Barese
- Will Janowitz as Finn DeTrolio
- Frances Ensemplare as Maria Nuccia Gualtieri
- Artie Pasquale as Burt Gervasi
- John Bianco as Gerry Torciano
- Louis Gross as Perry Annunziata
- John "Cha Cha" Ciarcia as Albie Cianflone
- William DeMeo as Jason Molinaro
- Angelo Massagli as Bobby Baccalieri, Jr.

- Miryam Coppersmith as Sophia Baccalieri
- Kimberly Laughlin and Brianna Laughlin as Domenica Baccalieri

Synopsis

Paulie begins the episode with expressing outrage at new policies implemented by the new priest, Father Jose, that will affect festivities at the Feast commemorating St. Elzear. Later on, however, Paulie's doctor calls and advises him to get a biopsy since he may have prostate cancer. .

At the feast, Adriana's mother Liz tries to convince Carmela that Christopher killed her daughter, a notion that Tony later disabuses her of, and Tony and Phil work out a deal regarding a shipment of vitamins hijacked by Tony's crew. Phil, in negotiations, insists that that Johnny Sack be left out of the profits.

During the parade, Father Jose's new policies—and Paulie's refusal adhere to them, as well as cutting corners on the festival budget, causes somewhat of a ruckus as people notice the missing gold hat. When there is an accident on a ride that injures women and children, Little Paulie is left to cope with the police investigation. Paulie continues to face a growing array of challenges as Bobby realizes Paulie did not spend enough money to ensure proper maintenance of the ride, Nucci tells him he has sinned for withholding said moneys for the ride, and Paulie deals with the fact that he needs to have a biopsy.

Christopher is also coping with his own set of challenges: when settling debts for the hit on Rusty, he decides to shoot up, and spends most of the time at the feast stoned and hanging out with a dog.

Later Christopher's girlfriend Kelli tells him that she is pregnant, and despite her offers to "take care of it", Chris enthusiastically suggests that they get married in Atlantic City. After they get married, Christopher goes to the Bada Bing wearing a wedding ring, but this does not deter him from feeling that he is still entitled to a bachelor party.

Christopher, despite a busy schedule impregnating his girlfriend and getting married, finds time to make a business trip to PA. When they pull over for a pit stop, they see two bikers stealing wine from a store, and end up stealing the wine from the thieves after a breif exchange of gunfire. They toast to their sucess at a restaurant, and Tony convinces Chris to fall of the wagon and drink to his new marriage.

After seeing a vision of the Virgin Mary at the Bada Bing, Paulie visits Nucci and watches television with her.

Trivia

- While awaiting the results of his biopsy, Paulie is shown awake 3:00am, an hour in the night that he is obsessed with.

- Christopher calls Tony "The Bad Lieutenant". In the film, the unnamed Lieutenant sees a vision of Christ just as Paulie sees a vision of the Virgin Mary, except the Lieutenant does not receive the revalation at a strip club.

- A cover version of "Pipeline", performed by Johnny Thunders, plays over the episode credits.

- The song playing throughout Christopher's high is "The Dolphins" by folk artist Fred Neil.

"Moe and Joe"

"Moe n' Joe" is the 75th episode of the HBO original series, The Sopranos. The episode was written by Matthew Weiner and was directed by Steve Shill. It was the 10th episode for the show's sixth season. It originally aired on May 14, 2006.

Guest Starring

- Cara Buono as Kelli Lombardo
- Carl Capotorto as Little Paulie Germani
- Arthur Nascarella as Carlo Gervasi
- Will Janowitz as Finn DeTrolio
- John Bianco as Gerry Torciano
- John "Cha Cha" Ciarcia as Albie Cianflone
- William DeMeo as Jason Molinaro
- Angelo Massagli as Bobby Baccalieri, Jr.
- Miryam Coppersmith as Sophia Baccalieri
- Kimberly Laughlin and Brianna Laughlin as Domenica Baccalieri
- Jeffrey M Marchetti as Peter "Bissel" De La Rosa
- Maureen Van Zandt as Gabriella Dante
- Danielle Di Vecchio as Barbara Giglione
- Ed Vassalo as Tom Giglione
- John Costelloe as Jim Witowski
- Denise Borino as Ginny Sacrimoni
- Cristin Milioti as Catherine Sacrimoni

- Caitlin Van Zandt as Allegra Sacrimoni
- Adam Mucci as Eric DeBenedetto
- Lou Martini Jr as Anthony Infante
- Brad Zimmerman as Ron Perse
- Rebecca Wisocky as Rene Cabot Moskowitz
- William Russ as Paul Calviac
- Patrick Holder as Earl Bretanoux
- Louis Mustillo as Sal Vitro

Synopsis

As the possibility of acquittal becomes more and more distant for Johny Sack, his lawyer advises him to flip. He scoffs at the suggestion so they decide to focus on a plea bargain, which, as a side effect, would mean that half of Johnny's assets would be frozen and then confiscated. Anthony Infante is dispatched to ask Tony to meet with two brothers from New Orleans who have a tacit contract with Johnny to share in owning a company together. Tony's task is to persuade them to sell the company so Johnny's share can be cashed out. Tony meets with them but one of the brothers is not swayed, and walks out of the meeting.

Tony's fee for engaging in this favor: he wants to buy Johnny's house on the cheap for Janice and Bobby. On top of organizing the whole Johnny Sack situation, Tony has to deal with Carmela pushing him again to meet with the building inspector on her property, and lean on him.

In therapy, Tony begins talking to Dr. Melfi about the relationships he has with the women in his life. He feels that Carmela's obsession with her spec house is infringing on her duties as wife and mother, and describes her as having a "don't ask don't tell" policy about his sexual encounter with other women. He also talks about how his relationship with his sister has changed through the years: as youngsters they were playmates, as she got older, boys and men would hang out with Tony just to get closer to his beautiful sister, and now, as an adult, she wishes to rest on her laurels and reap the benefits of his productivity. The latter, understandably, causes resentment and he is mean to her and Bobby as a result. It is after a session about Janice that Tony contacts Anthony Infante to tell him to sell the house to Janice. The gift leaves Janice in tears; however, he is stoic.

Later, a gang of black men mug Bobby him as he leaves a betting shop, and steal his collection money. Bobby escapes the encounter light of of his collection money, and, most likely, the sight in his right eye. Paulie calls Tony to discuss this, and discuss his health, telling Tony he is radiotherapy for early stage prostate cancer. After initially and unfairly expresing dissatisfaction with Bobby, Tony visits him at home and they watch a Giants game. Tony observes the broken furniture, Bobby's son's dismay that they can't get better satellite TV,and Janice's treatment of Bobby, Jr. with disapproval.

Tony arrives home to yet another woman with another problem: his daughter is concerned about the fate of her relationship with her fiance. She tries to discuss her sex life with him, which prompts him to try to send her off to talk to her mother. Upset, Meadow storms off and Tony is annoyed by the fact that his wife is not at home to deal with family matters such as this.

Landscaper Sal Vitro, however, has gotten some good news. He has doing free work at Johnny Sack's house for more than two years in return for maintaining the rest of his clientele. When Bobby and Janice take over ownership of the house, Tony informs him that he will no longer have to work for free at the residence.

In New Hampsire, Jim and Vito have moved in together, and Jim has finally realized that Vito is not, in fact, a writer. Vito, on the straight an narrow as a handyman, doesn't seem to fall in love with civilian life, living mostly for lunch breaks and weekends, and cooking Italian food on a regular basis. One night, realizing that his new peers are ready for bed at an hour when mobsters are ready to begin their evening, Vito takes his stuff from the apartment and splits, crashing into a parked jeep on the way back to Jersey. When the other driver attempts to call the police, Vito kills him and heads into the night.

Johnny Sack, meanwhile has recieved a fifteen year sentence. As part and parcel of the sentence, he has had to admit that he was part of La Cosa Nostra, and surrender a large portion of his assets.

Hits

- Car Accident Civilian: shot in the back of the head by Vito while attempting to call the police.

Trivia

- This episode marks the first time we see Tony getting the newspaper at the end of his driveway this season

"Kaisha"

"Kaisha" is the 77th episode of the HBO original series, The Sopranos. The episode was written by Terence Winter and David Chase & Matthew Weiner and was directed by Alan Taylor. It was the 12th episode for the show's sixth season. It originally aired on June 4, 2006.

Guest Starring

- Julianna Margulies as Julianna Skiff
- Cara Buono as Kelli Lombardo Moltisanti
- Arthur Nascarella as Carlo Gervasi
- Dania Ramirez as Blanca
- Lenny Venito as James "Murmur" Zancone
- Tom Alderidge as Hugh De Angelis
- Suzanne Shepherd as Mary De Angelis
- Denise Borino as Ginny Sacrimoni
- Angelo Massagli as Bobby Baccalieri, Jr.
- Miryam Coppersmith as Sophia Baccalieri
- Kimberly Laughlin and Brianna Laughlin as Domenica Baccalieri
- Geraldine LiBrandi as Patty Leotardo
- Kobi and Kadin George as Hector Selgado

Synopsis

Phil, accompanied by a young woman, is right in front of the Wire Room when a bomb goes off. He reports to Tony that everything went as planned, and Tony praises him for being so close to the store when it blew up, in order to avoid suspicion. Soon after, he finishes up a deal with Julianna and the cat and mouse game continues: he comes on to her and she declines.

Carmela returns home from visiting Adriana's mother in the hospital, where she is confined to her bed due to a suicide attempt, and tells Tony that Liz was upset by a letter from the Salvation Army, to whom Adriana made annual donations. Tony suggests that Liz is an alcoholic and Adriana couldn't stand her and moved away, so Liz should face facts. Carmela, however, smarts at this remark, and takes this opportunity to pressure Tony to help her expedite the process with her spec building by leaning on the inspector as he had promised. Tony puts her off. When she won't let Adriana's disappearance go, however, and threatens to call a private investigator, Tony gets his hustle on insofar as her spec project is concerned.

Christopher, meanwhile, is struggling with his new responsibilities as a husband and a father-to-be. He unable to muster as much enthusiasm as his wife when it comes to her pregnancy. To assuage his ennui, he has taken up with Julianna, who he met at an AA meeting she attended after Tony rejected her halfway through their makeout session. Christopher admits to Tony he has a comare, but since he knows that Tony will want to meet the comare he tells Tony it is a black girl named Kaisha that he can't bring around due to Paulie's racism.

Later, Little Carmine hosts a "meeting of minds" between New York and New Jersey. In attendance: Tony, Silvio, Phil, Gerry Torciano, and Butch DeConcini. Phil opens the meeting by insulting Vito, but Tony reminds Phil that Vito was one of his captains and always had impeccable earning ability. Phil brings up the "disappearance" of Fat Dom, who, as we see earlier in the episode, met a grisly end at the hands of Carlo Gervasi. Silvio and Tony feign knowing nothing about it, although they both approved the hit. Little Carmine indicates that the dispute is benefiting no one, and when Tony and Phil agree to a truce, Little Carmine mentions Phil's brother, which sends Phil into a fit. Phil leaves, after insulting both Tony and Little Carmine.

One evening, while having drinks with his coworkers, A.J. notices Blanca, an administrator from the construction site, and the two begin chatting. Despite learning that Blanca has a young son named Hector, A.J. asks for her phone number. Blanca gives it to him, but it is shy one number. She tells A.J. to find the missing digit on his own, and that way she'll know he's actually interested.

Apparently undeterred from first being ignored at the church festival, and then shut down after signing the Jamba Juice deal, Tony meets with Julianna at the warehouse and makes another move. She again says no, but this time, expresses annoyance with him. Later, Julianna and Christopher talk about his script and

Julianna asks whether the mob boss in the script is modeled after Tony. Christopher says that in a way, because both men think everything is theirs. He expresses reservations about indulging in sloppy seconds with Julianna, which upsets her because nothing has happened between her and Tony. Christopher points out that in Tony's mind, he has been there. She responds that she is "not a parking spot" before they have sex again.

Phil, still smarting from the meeting of the minds, discusses Tony with his captains Albie, Gerry, and Butch DeConcini. Butch wants to take a hit out on him, but when Phil doesn't like the idea, Butch then suggests picking "somebody over there".

After an AA meeting, Christopher meets with his sponsor, Murmur, and discusses the fact the Julianna and Tony have made out, but Murmur is more worried about the fact that Julianna has a history of drug and alcohol abuse. Christopher, however, feels that they can work together to avoid partaking in drugs and alcohol, instead of enabling eachother. Julianna has a similar conversation with her own sponsor, who says that Christopher, and those like him, are sociopaths.

As A.J. watches television with Blanca, a group of young men gather near her house and make noise and play loud music. She asks them to move since her son is sleeping, but they are unreceptive and cuss her out. She tells A.J. her ex used to beat them up, but he decides that it will be much easier to just bribe them with a mountain bike that his parents gave him. Later, in bed, A.J. asks whether their age difference bothers Blanca. It doesn't. She asks if the fact that she has a kid bothers AJ, and he responds that it doesn't.

Christopher visits Julianna with the intention of bringing her Robitussin for a serious cough. She thinks that it's a bad idea, however, to bring dextromethorphan into the house. A fare more acceptable alternative, she decides, is to bring 8-10 bags of Valerian tea into the house instead. 8-10 tea bags of Valerian is equivalent to a Valium. Christopher seems to agree and it's not long before tea bags have led them to freebase heroin in his car.

Back at the Soprano home, A.J. is putting up the Christmas tree when Carmela notices that a letter from the building department has come in the mail. The letter says that the stop work order on her spec house was lifted, and she thanks Tony exuberantly for his help.

At the Leotardo house, we learn that the housekeeper was Phil's companion on the night of the explosion at the Wire Room. Phil and his wife Patty are discussing holiday dinner plans when Phil complaina of chest pains and they quickly go to the emergency room. At the hospital, the doctor diagnoses Phil with gas, not a heart attack, but later that night, Phil wakes up hyperventilating, and his wife rushes him back to the hospital.

Murmur reports the news of Phil's heart attack to Tony, Silvio, and Paulie at the Bing. This news interrupted a hypothesis opined by Paulie, which was that he suffered erectile dysfunction because a girl he was recently trying to bang had on a Santa hat. The Santa hat, he concluded, was distracting and was the culprit for his inability to perform. Tony seems pleased with the news of Phil's heart attack and orders a round of drinks, but Silvio and Paulie point out that Phil had been a manageable problem, and any replacement could be harder to deal with. Tony disagrees, citing the meeting at Little Carmine's.

Bobby visits Junior at his care facility and returns the envelope full of money that Junior had given him as a Christmas gift. Bobby says he doens't feel right taking the money after what happend with Tony. Junior, in response, suggests that Tony may not have been acting alone, and that with the help of another patient in the instution who he refers to as his lawyer, he will mount an investigation. Bobby sadly leaves, and Junior gives the envelope to an orderly.

Down the street from Satriale's, Tony notices Christopher talking to Julianna in her car. He asks Christopher what the story is, and in response Christopher pretends that Julianna is friends with his imaginary black comare Kaisha after asking for Tony's version of what happened between them. Later, Christopher and Julianna discuss their complete and total control over their drug use over heroin, and Chris tells Julianna he has to tell Tony about her or Tony may find out that he's fallen off the wagon. At the Bing, Chris tells Tony the truth about his relationship with Julianna, saying he hid the relationship was that he was not sure how things had ended between him and Julianna. Tony appears stoic and says Christopher can do whatever he wants with her.

In therapy, however, a differnt story comes out. Tony tells Melfi he is angry because his fidelity costed him the woman he desired, and she wound up with Christopher. Dr. Melfi, always focusing on the positive, is happy that Tony did not turn to violence, and that he somehow realized that he doesnt have to have every woman he meets. Tony responds that all the women he has wanted, including Dr. Melfi, share certain characteristics, and that this must be the reason he continues seeing her, since he feels that therapy has changed little.

Agent Harris visits Satriale's and warns Tony him that Phil may be targeting someone close to him to avenge themselves in regards to recent events.

Christopher and Julianna, meanwhile, have changed their stance on their absolute control over their drug use. They discuss his taking omerta and that he is at odds with the higher-power heavy aspects of the program. She voices concern that is leaving her, but he denies it. She suggests they go to a meeting. Christopher reluctantly agrees tells her he will follow her in his car.

Tony visits Phil at the hospital in Brooklyn. Several of Phil's captains and soldiers are keeping vigil in the hallway, and Patty and Ginny Sacrimoni are at Phil's bedside. After they leave, Tony tells Phil about his coma, revealing that he went to a place that he never wants to visit again. Tony tells Phil to take his time recovering and enjoy his grandchildren and the good things in his life when he is better.

At home, Carmela discards the business card of the PI she wanted to hire to find Adriana, and Tony hopes that the spec house will be a distraction from that topic.. A.J. arrives for Christmas with Blanca and Hector. When out of earshot, voices disapproval of Blanca's age and race, but Tony seems glad his son is acting more grown up. The episode concludes with the entire extended family is gathered peacefully around the tree with Christmas music playing.

Trivia

- The episode was dedicated to the late John T. Patterson, who directed every season finale for the first five seasons and was a regular director.

- This episode is the second Christmas-themed episode with episode 3.10, ...To Save Us All From Satan's Power, being the first.

- The second part of the sixth season will follow in April 2007, dubbed Season 6B, as opposed to Season 6A respectively.

INDEX

Alan Taylor . 17, 95, 117, 127
Allen Coulter...... 33, 59
American Express....111
Andrew Schneider .. 95, 113
Atlantic City........ 13, 14
Bada Bing.....35, 43, 55, 57, 104, 119
Barone Sanitation....79, 97
Billy Madison............57
Bloomfield Avenue casino 71
Brooklyn 77, 79, 133
capos 12, 104
Coney Island 24
Crazy Horse 34
Da Giovanni............ 110
Danny Leiner 109
David Chase ... 2, 11, 59, 62, 68, 69, 83, 103, 127
David Nutter............. 83
Dean Martin 18
Diane Frolov 95, 113
DiMeo 56
Dr. Melfi. 13, 34, 43, 51, 55, 70, 101, 105, 106, 123, 133
dream.... 60, 61, 62, 80, 83, 85, 87, 92, 110
Emmy................. 68, 79

FBI ... 18, 19, 20, 34, 67, 71, 77
Florida 77
Frank Sinatra............18
Hamlet......................57
Hurricane Katrina ... 98
Ichabod Crane 57
Jack Bender 89
Jamba Juice............129
John Patterson ..21, 45, 69, 72
La Dolce Vita 47
Lupertazzi 11, 14, 17, 19, 20, 21, 31, 59, 60, 72, 79, 98, 112
made men 23
Matthew Weiner 17, 37, 50, 59, 89, 109, 121, 127
Miami.................13, 22
Michael Caleo 21
Michael Imperioli.... 45
Mike Figgis 54, 57
Mitchell Burgess 33, 54, 69, 103, 107
New Hampsire........124
New Jersey... 35, 51, 55, 67, 71, 106, 129
New Orleans 122
New York 12, 19, 22, 23, 25, 28, 29, 45, 55, 56, 66, 70, 71, 72, 102, 104, 129

Newark bridge 24
Peter Bogdanovich.. 37, 113
President Kennedy .. 42
Pulp Fiction 62
Robin Green 33, 54, 69, 103, 107
Rodrigo Garcia......... 27
Sammy Davis, Jr. 18
St. Vincent's Hospital 13
Steve Buscemi.... 15, 41, 57, 89, 92, 99
Steve Shill 121
suicide 67, 79, 128

Terence Winter ...11, 41, 50, 65, 68, 76, 79, 99, 103, 117, 127
The Godfather... 62, 63, 110
The Prince of Tides ...13
therapy. 25, 34, 70, 112, 123, 133
Tim Van Patten.. 11, 50, 65, 76, 103, 113
Toni Kalem . 27, 30, 45, 80
Valachi Papers 62

www.ingramcontent.com/pod-product-compliance
Lightning Source LLC
Chambersburg PA
CBHW032301150426
43195CB00008BA/534